Do's & Don'ts

of

House & Cottage Interiors

Written & Illustrated by

HUGH LANDER

ACANTHUS BOOKS

1982

Acknowledgements

I should like to say a special thank you to all the people who gave me the run of their varied and delightful houses to take photographs for this book. Their patience and good humour was exemplary. They moved pieces of furniture, climbed onto chairs to hold floodlights, spared hours of their time to discuss the architectural history of their buildings; and nourished me with coffee, tea, liquor and victuals.

Such handsome treatment was very greatly appreciated, and at the risk of lapsing into cliché, it is true to say that the book could never have been produced in this form without their splendid co-operation. — H.L.

Also By Hugh Lander

"Do's and Don'ts of House and Cottage Conversion".

A 32 page book, with a foreword by Alec Clifton-Taylor, deals in a similar form and format with questions concerning the exterior appearance of old buildings. It has more than seventy illustrations and is available from bookshops and from Acanthus Books, Lanner, Redruth, Cornwall.

Cottage fireplaces, like this Westmorland one of c.1700, can be surprisingly large and handsome. Note the corbelled jambstones, and their mouldings, which continue along the bottom edge of the lintel. This design clearly harks back to forms used in the late 15C (Fig 204) and earlier still. A simple but well proportioned classical cornice has been used, together with a carved simulation of a keystone.
A range has been fitted in the 19C which shows how the hob grate could finally develop into the mass produced kitchen range. This example has an oven on the left; but the front panels of the two hobs do not exactly match. Also, one hob slab is missing. Some believe that the hobs and panels are early 19C; while others think they may equate better with the 1840's. The chimney crane is possibly early 18C.

(Picture: Bill Brocklebank)

Cover Picture by **Eric Berry,** shows the massive granite open hearth of an early nineteenth century Cornish cottage.

CONTENTS

The hall of an ancient house with monastic origins. The cool simplicity of this interior embodies most people's ideas of how an old house should look and feel. Yet all too often they destroy the atmosphere by over modernisation or injudicious faking.

SAVING INTERIORS

When I was asked what this book would be about, my usual answer was: "How **not** to muck up the insides of old houses." After considering a number of more or less pompous paraphrases for that casual statement, I find it hard to improve upon its directness.

A great many fine words are both written and spoken regarding the importance of preserving the exterior appearance of old buildings. Planners, architects and conservationists, not to mention amateurs of discrimination, have now begun to demand higher standards when dealing with *exterior* features of the more obviously appealing old houses and cottages.

"Character must be preserved," they chorus piously. But what about the interiors of these buildings? Legislation as it now stands requires the owners of listed buildings to maintain the interior period features with no less care than the exterior facades. Yet throughout Britain, thousands of pleasant, and some priceless, old buildings are being ruthlessly stripped of everything which makes them worth living in.

These acts of vandalism may sometimes be carried out with "listed building consent" and at others are, strictly speaking, illegal.

* * * * *

Imagine yourself standing upon the pavement in some historic market town on a mild and sunny autumn morning. You are one of a group of officials and members of local amenity societies about to enter a fine brick 18th century merchant's house, which has recently been restored and saved for posterity.

You admire the excellent new slate roof, you wonder at the slavish skill with which the architects have researched and reproduced the pillared and pedimented doorway. You note with approval that the blank Victorian windows have now been replaced and given expression by the introduction of 12-pane sashes. Some clever fellow has even found a contemporary print to show how to re-fashion the cornice moulding beneath the parapet.

All concerned in this worthy project wear smiles of modest self-approbation. You enter the hall, and if you are the kind of person for whom this book has been written, the smiles will rapidly wilt into expressions of anguish.

The first thing you observe is that the open-well staircase, with cascading handrail and finely turned vase and column balusters, has disappeared. Some of the ceiling heights have been changed, and many cornice mouldings have been removed in the process.

The old panelled doors have been re-used, but now sport grisly, sherardized lever handles of aggressively modern design. All the new doors are of the flush variety — selected to meet the demands of a conscientious fire officer.

The inspection group, which by now, one hopes, contains a proportion of snorting dissenters, is led into the former drawing room. This is now the sanctum of the office manager, for most such centrally placed town houses become offices. His teakwood desk dominates a room devoid of almost all architectural details. Only the continued chimneypiece remains. Its graceful broken pediment now touches the combed and textured ceiling plaster, which is studded with electric downlighters, like converted cocoa tins. Above the desk dangles a numbing fluorescent light.

The chair rails have gone, and the window splays, where shutters once hung, are bare and featureless. The fireplace opening has been blanked off to preclude draughts, and a tastefully chosen switch-on Adam grate is flickering away with an air of dreadful complicity.

From room to room the position has worsened, like the embodiment of a threatening weather forecast. It started with sunny spells in the street outside, quicky became heavy showers as the tour progressed and culminates in a deep depression for those who recognise the enormity of what has been done.

"This," declares some bold and imprudent spirit, "has been turned into a modern house."

There is a general mutter of disapproval from other members of the conducted tour, who feel it is unmannerly to be critical in these circumstances.

"If we are to save old buildings like this, surely we must make it possible for owners to put them to some proper use," says the planning officer.

"But you don't have to take everything of any interest out to make it usable."

"You have got to remember that the building was in a serious state of dilapidation," says the surveyor.

"Yes, in a **dangerous** state," adds the owner's architect.

"I must say I rather take exception to your remarks," the office manager chips in. "We have spent a great deal of money on the building, and have worked in close liaison with the planning department at all times."

"We have bent over backwards to retain the character," agrees the planning officer.

"And you are over the moon?" suggests the dissenter bleakly.

"It had to be brought up to modern standards. People **do** have to earn their livings, you know," says the builder, more in sorrow than in anger.

The tour is to conclude with a buffet luncheon in the boardroom. You, the enlightened reader, and one or two kindred spirits, reluctantly forego these gastronomic pleasures, and flee to a nearby public house. There, as you discuss the iniquities you have seen, you quite forget to remark upon the fake oak beams above your heads, and the acres of far-from-Tudor carpet beneath your feet.

* * * * *

So what is the answer to the wider implications of that introductory scene? Let me think aloud as follows:-

— A great number of people like living in old buildings, or for reasons connected with their work, must take an informed interest in them.

— Many of them, however, do not know a great deal about the subtle details of interiors, which contribute to their enjoyment, or, in the case of some professionals, to that of their clients.

— A book which spells out some "Do's" and "Don'ts", leaving readers free to concur if they choose (but disregard at the peril of their own enjoyment) may well prove helpful.

— If somebody wishes to replace a feature which is missing, or introduce one which is in keeping, the answer seems to be a pattern book with photographs of typical details from different periods.

— Some readers may find a few of the architectural terms mystifying. The answer to that must be a fairly comprehensive glossary, and keyed photographs showing the parts of a room, a staircase and a door. (See page 17).

— Many people live in later houses of the Victorian and Edwardian periods and these too have special characteristics. They are none the less valuable to their owners for being rather recent in the scale of centuries. So illustrations must take account of later buildings.

— The older or more important the building, the better is the chance of an owner obtaining informed professional advice. Also documentary evidence and visual precedents are more likely to be readily available. This means that our book must not just be full of details from famous or grand houses.

— People visiting old houses open to the public, or inspecting more modest properties with a view to purchase, need a compact, but reasonably comprehensive book, from which they can glean information on the spot, or use when discussing details with their architect, builder or surveyor.

— Some points do not lend themselves to a bald statement of "do" or "don't". They require discussion or expansion and must therefore be touched on in subsequent pages. And, often, casting a long, dark shadow, are the Building Regulations.

Building Regulations and Fire Precautions

A new set of national Building Regulations finally came into effect in November 1985. Early in 1986, these same regulations superceded the old London building byelaws as well. For years, people involved in the repair, restoration and conversion of old buildings groaned under the burden of complex demands and prohibitions imposed by the 1966 regulations. Will the new approach prove any less punishing, especially as far as interiors are concerned?

There was always sense in the idea that methods of construction should conform with some reasonable standard of safety. Clearly, it was necessary to make sure that drains and waste pipes, ventilation and other factors related to health were properly properly monitored in some way. New work should obviously be of a kind which avoids any major fire risks. Yet most of us know from experience that the old regulations could make a nonsense of our carefully thought out plans to extend or rehabilitate old houses and cottages.

If the new regulations prove to have failed in all else, there is one vital change which must improve the chances of carrying out work which sympathises with the "character" of the original house. It is the sweeping away of that damnable requirement for a minimum ceiling height of 7′6″ and the equally damaging minimum clearance of nearly 6′7″ under beams, wherever the regulations applied. This meant that conversions, extensions and new work (which did not replace like with like), not to mention the replacement of floors and ceilings when grant aid was involved, all tended to drift you into the net. No longer is that the case.

Not much else appears changed for the better. Staircase regulations — old enemies of anyone trying to achieve authenticity — are very little different. Although rules for zones of open space have gone, there are still some potentially awkward provisos on ventilation.

The new regulations will have to be tested in practice, so it will be some time before we can tell if the more flexible terms in which they are written do, indeed, help those of us who want the best for old buildings.

The 1985 regulations are contained in a 62 page Manual, which gives the actual legislation, and says when they apply. As before, extensions, material changes of use (like barn conversions), and almost everything connected with drainage, plumbing, flues and fireplaces are regulated. The technical requirements set out in the old regulations are now embodied in eleven thin, staple-bound, "approved documents" ("A" to "L") which illustrate and explain methods which can be used to ensure compliance.

Perhaps the most important of these are "A" on Structure, "B" on Fire Spread and the additional mandatory document on "means of escape in case of fire"; if only because your work will be considered a "material alteration", and thus regulated, if it "adversely affects the building" as far as they are concerned. There is also a document dealing with materials and workmanship.

By implication, the new regulations are much more forgiving than the old ones, since they emphasise the idea that you are yourself responsible for complying. You do not *have* to do things by the methods advised in the approved documents; but to have done so will count in your favour if there is any dispute. If you can show that you are in line with the brief and rather general terms of the actual legislation while using *some other method* of your own, you are free to do so. However, it is stressed that by not following the approved documents, you will tend to compound any allegation that you have contravened.

The other major difference is that you can now choose whether you will subject yourself to the supervision of the local authority building inspectors, as before, or opt for an "approved inspector" paid by you on a private basis. But remember that the local authority inspectors are still the only ones who can dispense with or relax a regulation.

Fire Precautions

More and more fine old buildings, especially in towns, are now being used as hotels or offices. If more than a certain number of people occupy these buildings, they need fire certificates from the local authority to show they have satisfied their officers that the Fire Precautions Act of 1971 is being complied with.

The fire officers who inspect the buildings interpret the law by referring to the relevant codes of practice. If the owner, or his adviser, can make a telling case for leniency, the damaging visual effects may be considerably, but by no means entirely, mitigated.

At worst, if the fire officer is draconian or excessively cautious, or the owner unusually philistine, the architectural unity may be terribly impaired.

Old panelled doors are surfaced with fire retardant laminates, elegant landings screened off with unsuitable self-closing doors and fine staircases boxed-in.

It is too easy to apportion blame to those responsible for monitoring the Fire Precautions Act. Fire officers know that in the event of a disaster they will be put on the spot at any subsequent enquiry. "Why", they will be asked "did you not make sure that these people followed the codes of practice?"

This eventuality provides a powerful incentive for officers to be more or less wholesale in their demands. Owners, for their part, may be mean about spending money on difficult and costly works, when ugly methods are cheaper and will more easily procure them a certificate.

Perhaps the answer is an amendment to the law which would make it "self-enforcing", casting the onus upon the owner rather than the authority.

Certainly planning committees should be slow to grant 'changes of use' when it is clear that a building will have to be spoilt in the interests of fire safety.

It appears that the welfare state attitude to the citizen has now reached phobic levels of nannyish concern. The more sophisticated and speedy the emergency services become, the less we can be trusted to sleep safely in our beds in buildings which have withstood centuries of hazard.

There is no doubt that given the goodwill of all concerned, the bureaucratic tendency to ruin the insides of old houses could be checked, and the regulations and codes of practice vastly modified for the better.

Taste

There are few aspects of life which engender more resentment than those which hinge upon matters of taste. Just as most people believe that they have a sense of humour and are acute judges of character, there are not many who will admit to having positively bad taste or no taste at all. This is especially so when the taste is connected with a person's home.

Those who are willing to admit that they know nothing of machinery, music or making marmalade will become flinty-eyed if their taste in furniture or decoration is called in question. It seems to strike at the roots of their being. They believe that the mildest reservation about the way in which they have treated an old house fundamentally diminishes them as people.

This, of course, is nonsense. You may be kind and law-abiding, beautiful and funny, brave and responsible and still have no eye for how to set about reclaiming or altering the interior of an old building.

Conversely, some conceited and brutish fellow, who lets shop doors swing back on old ladies, and comes home to kick the cat, may have an unerring sense of visual propriety.

Professors will say: "It depends what you mean by 'taste'. Surely taste is subjective?" So it may be, but there is nothing inherently wrong in being subjective about old houses. In fact it is almost unavoidable. Too scholarly an approach can turn a building into a lifeless museum of antique styles.

Some neo-classical designers of the late 18th and early 19th centuries excelled at creating houses of a stereotyped grandeur — both heartless and devoid of spirit. You may admire without the remotest prospect of being seduced.

Each of us is a "purist" in some aspect of our life or work; but it is a label which we most readily apply to discriminating persons whose priorities differ from our own. As far as this book is concerned, "purism" will tend to mean adherence to the visual grammar of the period.

Grammar may sound off-putting, but a great writer, for example, may respect grammar without appearing to be a drab grammarian. It is, of course, a great deal safer and easier to be a grammarian when dealing with old houses, than to execute inspired *tours de forces* of decoration or design. Those who are capable of creating something beautiful or original, while remaining reasonably faithful to a building's general date and style, are providing a legacy for which future generations will bless them.

You only have to look at the incredible Rococo fantasies of the great German palaces and pilgrimage churches of the 18th century, where a riot of decoration smothers the classical serenity of the architectural orders, to see what you can get away with.

The dangerously dropped chunks of architrave and glowering rustication of 16th century Italian mannerists like Giulio Romano; or, closer to home, the naive, but vivid, combination of Renaissance and medieval imagery seen in some massive Elizabethan chimney-pieces, will prove again that grammar doesn't always rule.

In the 18th century nobody minded talking about taste, and they do not appear to have been short of that commodity, or of the robust sense of the ridiculous which prevents it becoming tiresome.

Today we could do with a lighter touch. We are too burdened by the self-conscious fear of seeming to be 'culture vultures'. Twentieth century Europeans are overwhelmed by so many conflicting emotions as far as their surroundings are concerned.

We find that an over-developed sense of guilt goes hand in hand with pomposity. A love of jargon vies with a liberal-minded desire to make all things simple, so that the veriest dunderhead may not feel under-privileged.

Those who inveigh against the idea of 'taste' itself are frequently shrewd enough to discern that it is an area in which they might fail to shine. They are inclined to murmur, with an air of ineffable smugness, such remarks as — "Wouldn't it be a pity if we all liked the same things."

This piece of gentle rhetoric is intended to allow the speaker to make a tactical retreat to higher moral ground, while conveying the notion that it is bad taste to discuss taste in the first place.

The real pity, I believe, is to be afraid of analysing, testing and questioning the reasons why we like or dislike what we see. By removing such matters from the arena of debate, we make it virtually impossible to learn anything new or to develop our abilities.

Dealing with the insides of old houses may not often be art with a capital 'A', but it is certainly an artistic pursuit as well as a technological one. No artist worth a damn can expect to produce good work unless he is professionally self-critical. However, it needs super-human discipline to be so in isolation. You are too close to what you are doing to seek out the imperfections.

Any enthusiast who writes about old buildings with conviction is almost sure to be accused of setting himself up as an arbiter of taste. Unless he has an unusually thick skin, this will hurt, for it suggests that he is unaware of the dangers of trying to deal in absolutes where often none exist.

What can be said is that to work effectively with old houses you must know something about the architecture, decoration and way of life in former times. You should also understand how buildings are put together from the constructional point of view.

Fashions and Improvisations

A banal statement, which I am particularly fond of making is "We are all creatures of our times." Indeed we **are**, as far as restoration and conversion work is concerned.

Nothing dates us more accurately, for instance, than the kind of staircase we choose to put in an old house. This has always been so. The man whose eye was trained in the twenties and thirties may find it hard to prevent the blonde finishes and fretwork patterns of that era from appearing in his designs. The cottages of those who began to mess about with old buildings in the sixties will sprout pirana pine ladder-like companionways. The seventies produced their crop of cast-iron, plastic and concrete spirals.

The 17th century gentleman ripped out his timber mast-newel stair and adopted the grandeur of an open-well, with turned balusters and ball finials.

To what extent should we all resist these impulses, and stick faithfully to the style of the building and the available evidence? I believe that we should design *new* interior details in fairly strict accordance with the predominant period features which remain in the rest of the room or the building.

However, there are going to be times when there is nothing to work from and we are obliged to improvise entirely for ourselves.

The points we then have to consider are as follows:

1. Is what we are doing correct for the period?

2. What materials should we use?

3. Will it be a pleasing example of its kind?

4. Are we using a feature which is likely to be too grand or of too high quality for the building?

5. Is the proposal too mundane — not grand enough?

6. Have we managed to keep it in scale?

7. Are the proportions convincing and easy on the eye?

8. What finishes, such as varnish, polish, paint, gilding or glaze may we have to employ?

The interior of an old house will have undergone numerous changes over the years. The owner, or his adviser, is set the tricky task of deciding what to rip out, what to restore, and what to copy or take as a theme for new work.

Professionals in the treatment of old buildings become exceedingly testy about issues of this nature. As among philosophers, cooks and slow-bowlers, there are various schools of thought. If this writer belongs to a particular one of these, the "Do's and Don'ts" pages which follow, will no doubt give him away.

Finally, we can only build up a visual sense which is based upon what other generations have habitually chosen to do. It is here that fashion enters the picture.

For example, if we are accustomed to William and Mary doors being painted white or left in their natural state and polished, it may come as a shock to see them artificially grained in the way many late 17th century owners favoured.

Brought up, perhaps, in a generation which associated that kind of thing with dreary municipal waiting rooms, we revolt at a practice which was once the height of fashion. Younger people, weaned on the nostalgia of the colour supplements, may like graining at once. They think of it as Victorian or Edwardian. To them it spells detail and craftsmanship, in an age of bleak and brutalist interiors.

Since fashion and necessity have more or less dictated the way in which houses were designed, decorated and furnished, there is no reason why we should not be discriminating in what we now do with them ourselves.

While it is deplorable if people lay waste original decorations which are rare and interesting, it must be admitted that not all of us would care to live in a castle where the inside walls are limewashed, and picked out in red lines to simulate coursed stonework.

Yet this is a genuine early form of interior decoration, dating back to the 13th Century. The practice of falsifying natural materials has been in and out of fashion for centuries. This fact does not always make it any more pleasing.

Nothing changes it seems, and the modern house owner, who papers the sitting room walls with a pattern of imitation brickwork, and the medieval lord with his simulated stonework may be brothers under the skin.

Comfort

There *are* people (some may even read this book) who believe that practicality must take precedence over appearance. This is not so. The inside of a house can retain the essential features of its period and still remain a perfectly comfortable place to live in.

However, there is no reason why physical comforts must always be uppermost in the choice of things like floor finishes, for example. That would be to deny the existence of other, and often more important comforts, like those to the eye, the touch or the mood.

In his book of the same name, Clive Bell remarks that the word "civilisation" does not just imply comfort. He goes on to explain that the most sybaritic societies were by no means always the most civilised. In 20th century Britain his views should strike a warning note.

An old house or cottage, which embraces you with an atmosphere of timeless well-being, may be far from comfortable in the superficial sense; and a materialistic young man from the estate agent's office may hesitate to describe it as a "luxury home".

All the same, it must be true that it is possible to obtain the best of both worlds by using a blend of architectural knowledge, practical common sense and a degree of low cunning. These, and a geniune feeling for old buildings, are the essential tools of the trade.

A good example is in the matter of double-glazing. There are occasions when this device may be virtually imperative. To fend off high levels of noise from traffic or aircraft, who can blame an old house owner for fitting some unobtrusive system of that kind?

In the majority of instances however, people with late 17th, 18th and 19th century houses may have an infinitely preferable method of keeping heat in at night and light out during the day — shutters. They look right and they feel right. To close the shutters at dusk on a chill December afternoon, and eat hot buttered toast in the firelight is an exquisite pleasure.

In summer, the shutters can be half closed to keep the light off the watercolours, and on golden afternoons you may doze in sub-aqueous gloom after a heavy luncheon.

Carpets

This book is really intended to deal with architectural matters, rather than those which might be described as furnishing or decoration. Generally speaking, the latter can be changed at any time in the future without damaging or drastically altering the building. However, the treatment of floors has a massive effect upon the appearance of an old building and is too important to avoid some discussion.

It is sometimes objected that the polishing of floors is a very strenuous occupation for busy modern wives. There are two answers to that contention. In the first place, only a zealot polishes floors or brasses more than once a month, though they might conceivably pay someone else to do so. Secondly, whoever said that this duty must necessarily be allotted to women? Men are ideally adapted to these mundane tasks, and floor polishing should be mandatory for gentlemen with spreading waist lines.

Some harsh words are written about fitted carpets in this book. I believe that patterned carpet of this kind is usually busy and unpleasing. It detracts from intrinsic details of the interior, such as plasterwork, and does little to set off furniture to advantage. It is also too expensive to abandon if changes of fabrics or colours are planned.

Plain Wilton fitted carpet, though less demanding and undoubtedly warm and luxurious, tends to look modern and can convey a feeling of claustrophobia. Fine antique furniture standing upon thick fitted carpets calls to mind the velvet lining of a jewellery box. Those polished and mellow pieces are made to appear temporary and improbable — eternally waiting for somebody to unpack them and set them genuinely to work.

Obviously these sentiments may prove unpopular with a very great number of people.

For some reason, fitted Wilton looks far less out of place in bedrooms than it does downstairs, or in halls and landings. This is perhaps because the mind has subconsciously accepted softer and more sybaritic values for places where you sleep. However it only requires some exposed and polished boards in the window recesses to remind you that you are walking upon the floor of an old building.

Here it should be added — and this may be thought contrary — that some of the more successful fitted floor coverings for use in old houses and cottages are the many neutral coloured variations of haircord. They provide warmth, deaden sound and make an inoffensive background for oriental rugs, which paradoxically appear to go with anything.

So on the whole, the answer seems to be an 18 inch to 24 inch border of plain polished floor on as many sides of the room as possible. It is a view with which some people may disagree, and I would not go to the stake for it.

Finally, on fitted carpet, lest I be accused of not paying attention to history, it is known that patterned pieces were being sewn together to cover the whole floor area, as early as the 18th century. However, the relentless visual clamour and vulgarity of most modern broadloom should make us beware.

To be fair, we must remind ourselves that the much-prized antique carpets, which we sometimes see in fine houses, have been greatly mellowed by the passage of the years. It would be interesting to know what our reactions would have been to a bright and brand new Savonnerie carpet, covered with gilded Louis Quinze furniture if we could step back in time.

Inventions Ancient and Modern

In each era of a building's history, the owners will make improvements using the fashions and technical discoveries of the day. Houses are subtly, and not so subtly, changed and amended as time goes by. The big down-hearth, burning huge logs, is replaced by a dog-grate with a basket, and eventually by a hob-grate. Oil lamps take over from candelabra and wall sconces when the punitive restrictions backing up the candle tax of 1709 are lifted in 1831.

Before that only lamps burning stinking fish oil were permitted. People therefore used rush lights and candles; but the latter were employed far more sparingly than might now be supposed.

Where do you draw the line therefore, between what was correct for 1781 and what is feasible in the 1980's? You are not demanding that we abandon electricity, for heaven's sake you will be saying? Do we have to strip out the wiring along with the Axminster, you cry in exasperation.

Of course not, even if I dared suggest it, I should not want to.

Running water, refrigerators, deep freezers, electric kettles and television are some of the benefits of not living in the 18th century. None, except television, it will be noted, are aesthetic boons, but they are splendidly practical.

It would be a hard man indeed who did not enjoy a spaghetti western on T.V.; an hour in a hot bath with a good novel, the pleasure of a glass of chilled hock, or a mug of hot sweet tea for that matter. It is just that the means of purveying these delights can still be made as unobtrusive as possible.

Kitchens

Kitchens are especially vital. They are often the one room in which an otherwise discriminating house-owner surrounds himself, or herself, with a plethora of synthetic-looking fixtures and finishes.

Why should the kitchen be relegated to the position of a bright and boring laboratory for cooking and washing-up? It is probably, of all rooms in the house, the one in most constant use. It should have pictures and attractive curtains and objects to please and divert the eye. Much of the natural clutter of a kitchen can do exactly that — copper pans, robust and colourful china, and all the wood and steel and enamel paraphanalia for cooking and serving food.

There are people who argue that it is in some way morally unsound to disguise the equipment of modern living. When dealing with old buildings morality is nothing to do with the case. The values are aesthetic and pleasure seeking. There are no prizes in this world, or the next, for those who make a fettish of that kind of 'honesty'.

Our Georgian ancestors knew it when they refrained from displaying the chamber pot, and concealed it in an elegant little mahogany stand with cross banding, tapered legs and brass handles.

Decoration is often involved with disguise, and what counts is success. Just as the law will apprehend the clumsy criminal whose false beard falls off as he makes his escape, so shall the ill-conceived tricks of the inept house decorator and improver bring about their own form of nemesis.

The hacked and stained softwood boards, which hide that steel universal beam, shout "fake" when seen beside their ancient, adzed and chamfered neighbours. In other words, if you are going to fake something in an old building, you had better make a very good job of it. If you can't be good, be clever.

All this applies to rooms in any part of an old building. It is realised that these admonitions will irritate the archaelogically-minded and I sympathise with them. All of us who spend our time trying to piece together the visual evidence which helps to date old houses, are far from pleased to find that what we took to be an original chimneypiece, has been artfully and convincingly devised by the present owner.

We should really be delighted that the building is being given that degree of educated attention.

Lighting

There are a few points to bear in mind about lighting in old houses. Some run counter to the fashion of recent years. First is the fluorescent light.

On no account should fluorescent lighting be used anywhere in an old house, unless it is totally hidden from view; and that definitely includes the kitchen. They are hard, graceless abominations and kill the atmosphere of any room with relentless efficiency.

There may sometimes be a case for putting such lights in concealed positions to illuminate architectural features, since they run cool compared with filament bulbs. Obviously they can also serve in a workshop, but that *does not* include an office in an old house. I believe this with such fervour that I do not care how unpopular it makes me, even with loved and respected friends who already have them.

The second bête noir is the suspended ceiling light. While there are rooms, and perhaps kitchens are among them, in which ceiling lights may prove harmless, or even effective, they are usually a menace in old houses.

It is almost impossible to find a shade which suitably alleviates the nightmare quality of this type of overhead lighting. Where, through idleness or ineptitude, one has settled for a suspended bulb light, the favoured method of mitigation is to buy a chinese paper lantern to cover it. That helps.

Sometimes a converted 18th century lantern looks well in a hall; but like electrified chandeliers and oil lamps they are seldom entirely successful when switched on.

Wall sconces never cease to cry out for real candles, and should the electrified variety be fitted with shades, they leave us mentally marking our own card: "Can do better."

The only satisfactory way of lighting a room with electricity is to have individual lamps scattered around on tables and other likely pieces of furniture. Obviously, the prettier the lamp base and shade, the better the whole room will look. The fact that this kind of lighting is set low, makes it soft, interesting and perfectly practical. If you want to read, or write, or sew a sampler, you sit near the light.

For this type of lighting, it is, of course, necessary to have one of the wall sockets switched at the door to put on when you enter the room.

In old houses the use of spotlights is an anachronism. Also downlighters, set in the ceilings of old rooms, especially the more formal ones with plaster mouldings, are nothing short of vandalism. It was a fashion of the sixties and seventies. One prays that the eighties will see the last of both these forms of lighting in old buildings.

Uplighters — those things like metal waster-paper bins with electric light bulbs in them — can provide dramatic lighting which may sometimes look well. The trick seems to be to hide them behind bulky chairs or sofas.

Standard lamps are really furniture and many are horrid. Some are artfully contrived from 18th century bedposts, and with well-chosen shades appear to commend themselves. It is a matter of whether you happen to like them.

This is an area of opinion rather than assertion. Standard lamps? You may pop them in or chuck them out at will. But it is reasonable to claim that downlighters in a rococo ceiling provide a straightforward way of ruining an old room.

Colour

You may be relieved to hear that it is impossible to make hard and fast rules about the use of colour in old houses. For this reason the subject has not been given a section among the "Do's and Don'ts" which follow.

The whole matter is exceedingly complex. From the historical point of view, surviving examples of original decoration are usually faded and often damaged, making it difficult to know exactly what they looked like when they were fresh and new. Apparent contradictions of style abound, and contemporary letters and records tend to confuse matters even further.

Everybody sees colour differently, and on top of that, we only have verbal descriptions in most cases. It's anybody's guess quite what a letter writer meant by "dove grey" or "pea green". Such comparisons often turn out in the last event to be astoundingly far from the reality if a sample of the original colour is found in mint condition.

To deal adequately with the niceties of colour is far outside the scope of this book; but we can discuss a few general principles which may help. Here then are some points to bear in mind.

The first important one is this. Are we trying to restore an actual scheme on the basis of existing evidence, or creating a speculative design based on the manner of other existing examples? Or are we just using colour in a way which we think will look well? All these approaches are perfectly legitimate.

Next we must decide what materials we can use. It is a major undertaking, which requires skill and research to try to reproduce the natural pigments and media used in former times. Only very early houses of great interest or quality will usually merit this kind of treatment.

If we are to use modern paints, as most people normally do, it is sometimes necessary to decide whether or not to employ special brushwork techniques, like dragging, and stippling. There may be a case in an 18th century house of presence to attempt the subtle glazes favoured in that period. For these, very thin top coats were painted over paler grounds which glowed through, giving life and variety to the effect. This has always been a traditional method used by the artist in oils to build up a picture.

Yet again, we must consider whether we could live with some of the more garish colours and designs used in the past. They can be correct, but also ugly and disquieting.

The use of varnishes leaves us with a number of questions to answer. As a rule their modern application to surfaces in old buildings is disastrous. Varnish of almost any kind has a tendency to make everything it touches look harsh and spurious.

Against this must be set the fact that varnishes were constantly used in previous ages. For instance, special effects like marbelling and graining, which were fashionable in the late 17th and 18th centuries, were usually varnished to give them protection and lustre. Alas, steel rim locks were often varnished in the 18th Century. The use of varnish on stained pine during the late Victorian and Edwardian periods will be familiar to most people, as it is the favourite finish in the majority of older town halls and public libraries.

The conclusion we can draw from all this seems to be as follows. We now have a more extensive range of easily applied paints and colours than has ever been known before. We might as well use them to advantage. However, some look better in old buildings than others.

My own view is that flat emulsion paints and egg-shell finishes are usually preferable to gloss when large areas have to be dealt with. There is no harm in employing white, or broken-white, gloss to the woodwork of doors, chair rails, skirtings and so on; but the fashion of late has been to use flat paint for these and for panelling.

Flat paints were extensively used in the 18th century in the form of water based distempers. Oil paints too were given a matt finish by applying a "flatting" coat made with turpentine.

I believe that old softwood wainscotting looks better painted in rather quiet, flat colour washes. These are tranquil to live with and set off furniture and pictures – they do not look greasy, or yellowed with time.

In grand houses with classical mouldings it may be both correct and attractive to pick out parts of the detail in gold. Since this should be done with gold leaf and **not** paint, it is better to forget the idea altogether than to do it badly. Flat colour paints can also be used for picking out, but all this requires the most excellent judgement, coupled with some understanding of the classical orders. It may often be wiser to play safe and use white, or broken white only, for entablatures and similar architectural components.

Well-chosen colour washes may be applied to the general background areas such as walls and some ceilings, while decorative plaster details like swags, trophies, arabesques, garlands, wreaths and surrounding mouldings should be flat white.

Everybody can point to examples where ceiling mouldings — in say a Palladian house — have been cleverly treated with subtle tinted washes; but unless you are knowledgeable, have both good colour sense and a flair for decoration, you might do better to play safe with white.

Should you have a Tudor, Elizabethan or Jacobean ceiling, which requires extensive use of colour to enrich strapwork or bosses, seek expert advice. You may otherwise find that your best endeavours leave the place looking like an aggressively *Jacobethan* roadhouse.

Whatever the traditional practices of the past, you can seldom go wrong if you wax polish the surface of any woodwork which is to be left in its natural state. This is not to preclude the cautious use of some mild colouring agent to give richness to ordinary softwood when it is new, for instance. Carry out test pieces to make quite sure that you are not going wrong. Many modern stains can look extremely fierce and, once applied, are virtually impossible to remove.

Any woodwork with veneers should always be wax polished only.

Never, on any account, pick out the detail of ironwork on staircases in pastel colours, or gold paint. Iron balustrading should almost always be either black or white in a flat paint. Any enrichment should be gilded. Gloss finishes for interior ironwork have a way of appearing sticky and unwholesome. The matter is debatable, but look about you and see if you agree that many lovely 18th and 19th century staircases are ruined by the insensitive way in which they are painted. The best places to see this exemplified are the many hotels and coaching inns which have suffered from generations of unsympathetic "improvers".

* * * * *

PARTS OF A ROOM

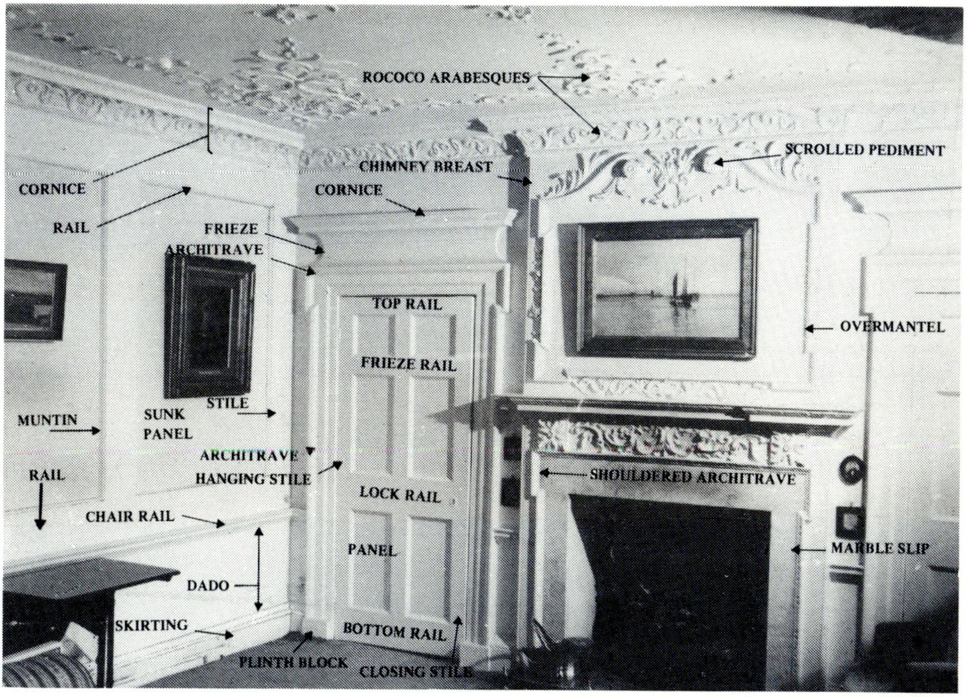

PARTS OF A STAIRCASE

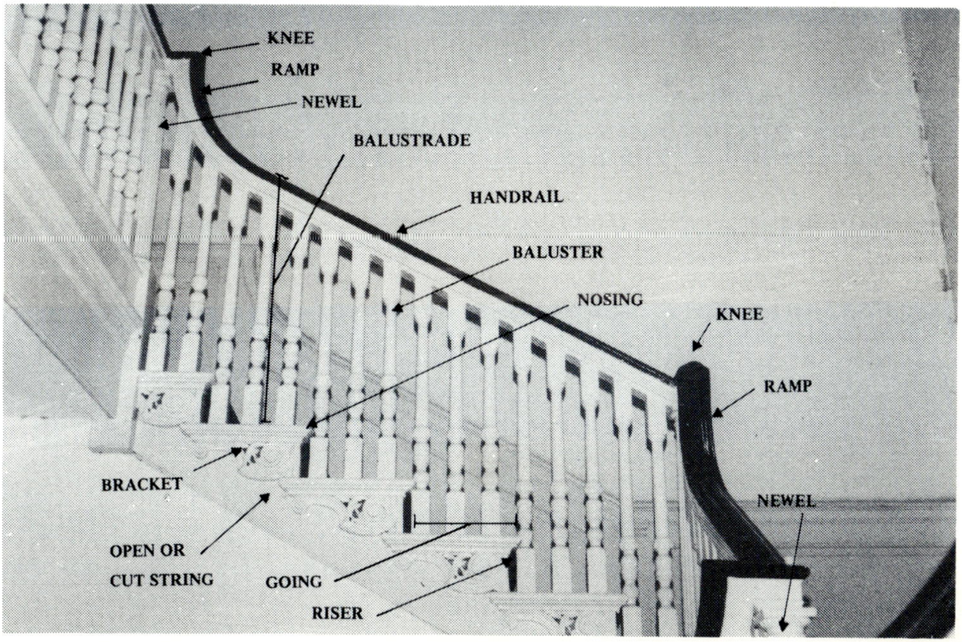

MOULDINGS

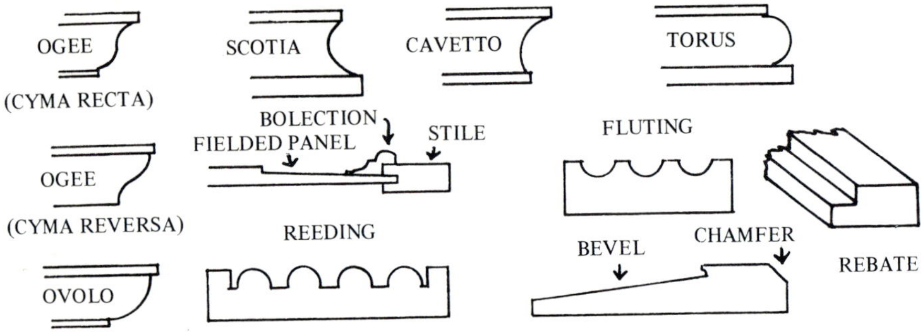

The outlines of some of the most commonly used mouldings, shown in cross-section

THE TUSCAN ORDER

NOTE:

The Renaissance version of the Tuscan Order has been shown here to illustrate the basic points relating to interiors. However, it is necessary to study all five main orders to understand something of the influences at work in the designs of former eras.

Although the Tuscan Order is seldom seen in its entirety, inside buildings, it is the simplest; and its cornice relates best to many of those which you will find in old houses of the late 17th. and much of the 18th. centuries.

For the last four hundred years, English architects and craftsmen have mixed-up, altered and adapted the orders with a fine disregard for the pattern book versions of Serlio, Vignola, Palladio, Perrault, Gibbs and Chambers. German and Flemish treatises of the 16th. century were especially idiosyncratic and set off the exuberant fantasies to be found in Elizabethan and Jacobean houses.

Those readers who wish to pursue the matter will gain much innocent amusement, and not a little frustration, in trying to equate the pattern book orders with what they actually see in old buildings.

THE TUSCAN ORDER

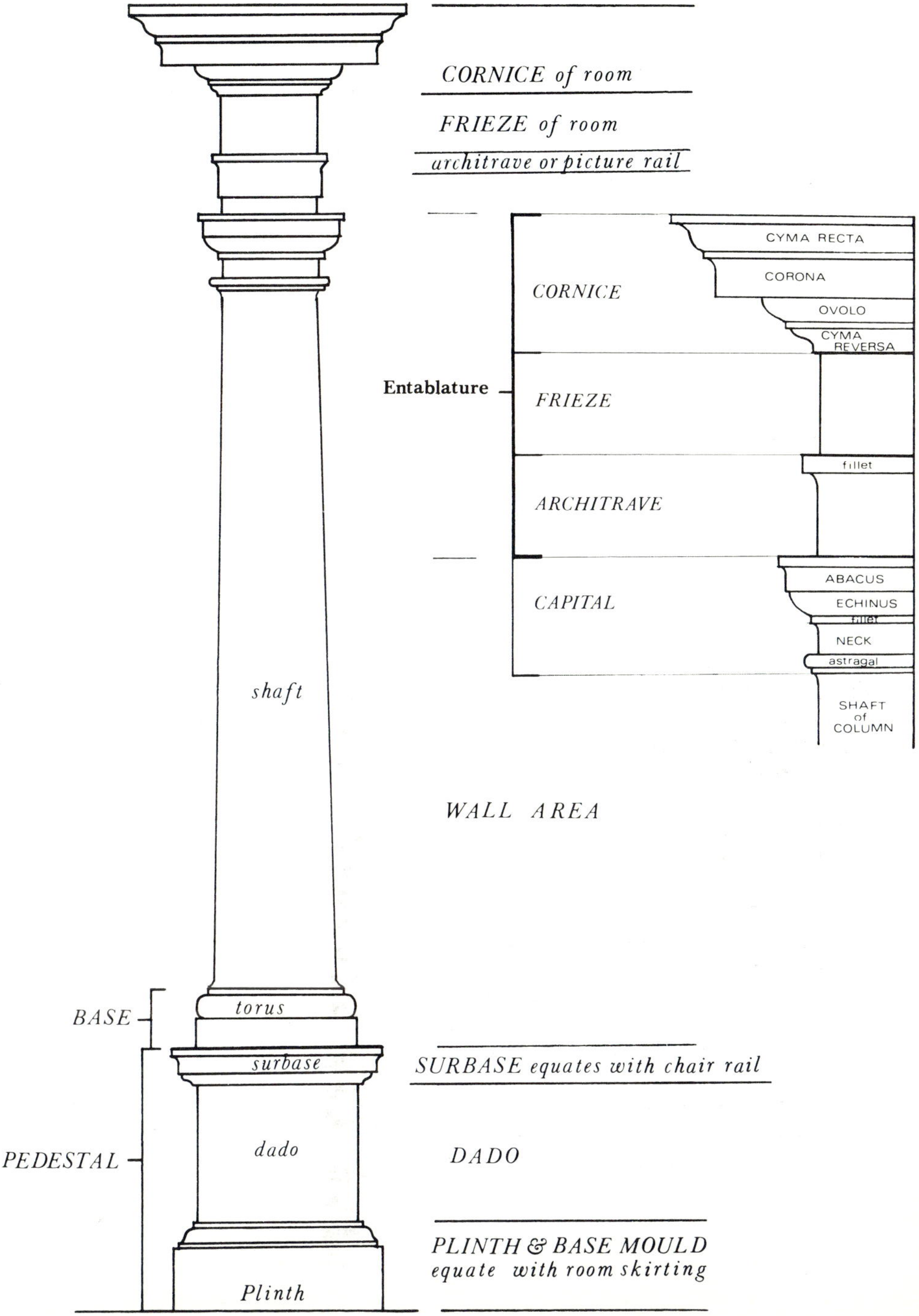

The Do's and Don'ts

All the advice listed in the sections below should be followed selectively, with due regard for the date, style, quality and atmosphere of the building you have in mind.

WALLS AND WINDOWS

Don'ts

1. Don't take down original internal walls and partitions of formally designed houses. By doing so you can ruin the proportion of rooms and cut into wall and ceiling mouldings. **Note**: There is a very good case in the smaller type of cottagey property for knocking two tiny rooms into one reasonable size living room. However, a good deal of discretion should be exercised in deciding which house can bear this kind of treatment.

2. Don't be too hasty in any work connected with an old house — if you think you have found something interesting (like a wall painting or concealed window) call in an expert before any work starts.

3. Don't remove old panelling — this is fundamental to the character of the house, and is protected anyway if the building is listed.

4. Don't remove original chair rails or skirtings unless they are too rotten to save. Then you must replace them in the same manner.

5. Don't on any account remove original cornices, friezes or other plaster details.

6. Don't take out original timber or plaster niches — they serve a useful and decorative purpose. With listed buildings it will normally be illegal to do so without consent.

7. Don't carry out imitations of period panelling, arches, cornices and other details unless you can do so correctly. Nothing looks worse than a thoroughly vulgar pastiche.

8. Don't expose and point large areas of stonework, which were clearly intended to be plastered. Very few old buildings had bare stone walls.

9. Don't erect partition walls in unsympathetic materials which do not blend with the original rooms; or introduce them in such a way that they cut into old wall and cornice mouldings.

10. Don't, on any account, partition a room or area in such a way that you leave no visually adequate pieces of return wall alongside window or door openings. The returns at these openings should be at least wide enough not to look cramped, and it may be worth making them sufficiently generous to allow a piece of furniture to stand against them. Of course, when cutting openings in old cottages this ideal may prove impossible in practice. **Note**: It is appreciated that it was quite common in late 17th and early 18th century houses, where one room leads into another along one side, to find that the original builders made exactly this mistake.

11. Don't, in rambling, cottagey properties allow craftsmen to plaster walls with sharp, straight arrises and hard smooth finishes. Also avoid giving plaster unsuitable modern textured, combed, patterned or granular finishes.

12. Don't cover original structural wall timbers with dark Tudoresque paints and stains.

13. Don't use any kind of simulated timber wall covering.

14. Don't use v-jointed tongue and groove boarding without very carefully considering its suitability. Timber linings of t & g (v-jointed or otherwise) are traditional in many Scottish buildings, like shooting or fishing lodges. They would be most inappropriate, however, in one of the main rooms of a house which has any pretensions to formality.

15. Don't use varnish or polyurethane sealers or finishes on any woodwork, with the possible exception of that in some Victorian and Edwardian buildings, or to protect special decorative effects like marbling and graining.

16. Don't seal exposed interior stonework or bricks with clear varnish-like solutions of any kind.

17. Don't apply plastic and other forms of unsympathetic wall tiles and panels to walls of old buildings.

18. Don't cover the walls of old rooms with acres of mirror glass, despite Versailles and the Amalienburg pavilion at Nymphenburg. Hotels and restaurants, please note.

19. Don't use harsh or contemporary looking paint colours in old houses. Choosing and mixing colours is certainly very difficult, but you should aim for subtlety, even at the cost of much trial and error (see pages 14, 15 and 16)

20. Don't use wallpapers with modern looking designs in old houses. If necessary go to a specialist firm with good pattern books, and get help with your choice. The right paper can make or break a room.

21. Don't choose outlandishly modern patterns for your curtains if you wish to create an atmosphere in keeping with the feeling of an old house. Study books on interior decoration, and co-ordinate your curtain colours, patterns and style with the rest of the room. Unless you have exceptional flair, it is best to be gentle in your choices of colour, pattern and texture.

22. Don't stick or nail back old shutters so they cannot be used.

23. Don't remove old original shutter catches, handles or bars.

24. Don't use flock-type wallpapers in rooms which are clearly not formal enough to merit them — in the dining room of a cottagey pub for example.

WALLS AND WINDOWS

Do's

1. Do, where structural repairs etc. demand the removal of interior features, carefully measure and record before starting the work. It is important that everything goes back in its original place, and in its original form. Naturally this care will be in ratio to the age and/or quality of the building.

2. Do tap, probe and investigate wall surfaces for the possible presence of concealed fireplaces, blocked up windows and doors. Even if you do not wish to restore them, it is interesting to know where they were and how the house was organised in former times. That in Fig 10 should clearly have been repaired and kept as a window.

3. Do retain all old panelling, chair rails, skirtings and pilasters.

4. Do remember that houses of the 17th century or earlier may contain important panelling which has been concealed. For example, look out for signs of timber partition work which may have once formed the screens passage to a medieval open hall.

5. Do keep any original alcoves, recesses, plaster or wooden niches, retaining or restoring the mouldings where necessary. These will usually prove to be either late 17th century, or more likely 18th or early 19th century.

6. Do retain any cupboards and their doors and mouldings if they appear to be characteristic of the room. Figs 35—39.

7. Do retain old skirting boards (Fig 20), and repair or replace with due attention to the details of the originals. **Note**: It is very difficult to lay down a rule of thumb for designing skirtings, since practices varied according to the quality of the building and its period. However, it is worth obtaining boards of reasonably generous dimensions even for cottages, i.e. 6″ x 1″ minimum. These may be embellished with a simple stuck or planted moulding along the top edge. Skirtings of 19th century houses, particularly, were often of considerable height, being built up in sections. Fig 29.

8. Do consider the use of tiles to form a skirting, especially in kitchens, laundries, still rooms, sculleries, pantries and bathrooms. In 17th century Dutch houses, excellent use was made of this device (employing 'Delft' tiles) — see paintings by Vermeer and De Hooch.

9. Do look out for original faux bois and faux marbre effects on skirtings and panelling, especially if your house is late 17th or 18th century. Fig 26.

10. Do keep old matchboard partitions or wall linings where they are appropriate to the period of the room. They are often found in 19th century cottages. Sometimes, however, these will be too decayed to be worth saving.

11. Do strip wallpapers with care to ensure the possibility of saving any period papers which may be concealed beneath them. Genuine papers from the Regency, the 18th century, or better still the 17th century, are of great interest and are prized accordingly. (see illustration p42)

12. Do look out for "jib doors" in the panelling of rooms, and free them if necessary. They may reveal something interesting about your house, and could be useful and diverting. Fig 155.

13. Do preserve any original wall paintings, murals or trompe l'oeil decoration. Post and plank partitions in medieval or Elizabethan houses may reveal decorative painted designs of variety and interest; if you are very lucky. If these, and any mouldings, finish 18″ or so short of the floor, there may have been a bench seat which has been removed.

14. Do research carefully any signs of decorative carving, however crude, as it may be important to the room's period or development.

15. Do, where stonework is to be left exposed, clean it, rake out the joints and point it correctly. **Note**: Pointing should be kept well back from the edges of the stones, and should be carried out in a weak lime:cement:coarse sand mortar, approximately 1:2:9. The mortar should be brushed just before it goes off to give it texture, and should have a colour which blends quietly with the stonework. Fig 33

16. Do, in rough cottages, barn conversions, etc., employ the whitewashed look (Fig 34) or use a cross-grained wood float to texture new plaster before it sets. The mix should be weak and preferably contain lime — say, cement/lime/coarse sand proportioned 1:2:9. The plaster should undulate very slightly, following the natural contours of the wall. External and internal corners should be blunted and allowed to wander, just a little. It is vital, however, that these measures do not look contrived.

17. Do, where exposed stonework must be repaired or replaced, find old stone of the right type, size and finish. If you patch with new stone **inside** a building, however much it pleases the archaeologists, it will not tone down much in your lifetime.
This is a controversial point amongst experts, and some authorities, such as the Society for the Protection of Ancient Buildings, tend to the view that new work of this kind should be seen for what it is. It is arguable whether new stonework should be distressed. Perhaps it depends on how cleverly it is done; but on the whole, it is better to leave well alone.

18. Do retain any old crown or muff glass in sash or casement windows. It's imperfect texture is very attractive. Diamond or rectangular leaded panes in 16th or 17th century casements will usually be extremely thin and may have a greeny or grey colour. Do also look out for diamond scratched names, initials or messages on window panes. They may just say "Kilroy was here", but you *could* find the signature of some illustrious former occupant or visitor. Figs 10 & 17.

19. Do uncover or free any old internal shutters which have been pinned back to window splays. Also retain attendant panelling and mouldings, or any period splay or soffit panels. (Figs 7 & 8). Shutters which can be used are of inestimable value on three counts — aesthetic, insulation and security.

20. Do clean up, expose or reinstate any old window boards (interior sills). They may look rough, but could be of original interest.

21. Do keep an eye open for old window seats which have been built up or concealed at a later date. A window seat is practical and pleasurable in equal measures.

22. Do avoid the use of modern wrought-iron grilles, gates, brackets and sconces etc, as a general rule. These all to often end up looking like features from a Hollywood costume epic; or they infect the house with an unwelcome touch of the haciendas.

Don't leave or introduce pieces of exposed stone sticking out of plastered walls, in an attempt to fake a sense of age and character. They neither charm nor enlighten.

This ancient window, with its hollow chamfered granite mullions and Tudor-headed lights, is set in the massively thick walls of the tower of an early 16C. house. The lead glazing is set in a pattern more often seen in the 17C. The sockets in the window jambs were, no doubt, for housing the ends of stout timber shutter bars.

CEILINGS AND CORNICES

1. Don't remove old plaster ceilings and their mouldings unless they are beyond practical salvation, and even then, if they are of some quality, consider having them copied.

2. Don't remove ceiling coves or cornices. These are usually essential, especially in formal houses, to make the visual jump from the vertical to the horizontal plane.

3. Don't introduce ceilings at new levels which spoil the proportions of rooms. To do so can mean a loss of wall height over window and door openings, which is visually destructive. It may also make the use of curtain pelmets, valances or poles very difficult.

4. Don't square up old, sloping cottage or garret 'camp' ceilings. They usually contribute to the period character of the rooms.

5. Don't use any of the modern ceiling board finishes in old houses. This includes modern ceiling tiles and panels of various shapes, sizes and textures. (Ordinary plasterboard, designed to have a plain, skimmed finish, is perfectly acceptable in most instances).

6. Don't cover old plaster ceilings with tongue and groove boards, as a general rule. Some rooms in houses of late 19th and early 20th century vintage, if especially ugly, may occasionally benefit from such measures.

7. Don't, if using t & g boards seal them with polyurethane, or give them any kind of varnish finish. Especially in cottages, consider white emulsion paint on t & g. In Victorian or Edwardian lodge-type buildings, varnish, though repugnant, may be correct.

8. Don't stick fibrous plaster or anaglypta mouldings to old ceilings without careful research into the type and quality of detail that such a ceiling might be expected to have. This is not an easy matter. **Note**: A form of papier-mâché ceiling decoration was in fact used in the late 18th century, and there is nothing inherently wrong in applying modern fibrous cast details to ceilings, provided that they are of the correct pattern. However, this is an area where research, and possibly expert advice, is necessary.

9. Don't imagine that the stock fibrous cornice mouldings at present on the market are necessarily right for your home, just because they are described as eighteenth century. They may be suitable for one Georgian house, but quite wrong for another.

10. Don't plaster old ceilings and then apply any of the obnoxious combed and textured modern finishes.

11. Don't use textured papers of modern design on ceilings of old buildings.

12. Don't be afraid to use an all-over patterned paper on sloping garret ceilings. It requires taste, luck or good judgement, but can be most successful.

13. Don't paint old ceiling mouldings in colours which take your fancy, without regard to the period of the plasterwork. (See also, pages 14, 15, 16)

14. Don't go mad with the gold paint on the detail of 18th and 19th century ceilings. The amount of picking out of this kind will depend upon the date and style of the plasterwork. Eighteenth century plasterwork was decorated with real gold leaf — nowadays financially prohibitive for most people.

15. Don't suspend a modern pendant light flex from a plaster or decorative wood ceiling boss, intended for a chandelier.

16. Don't insert downlighter fittings, ventilator panels, loudspeakers etc. in old plaster ceilings.

17. Don't, on any account, use fluorescent lighting in old houses. Nothing so quickly introduces a harsh, modern note. There is occasionally a place for this type of lighting, if it is totally concealed, as a means of illuminating architectural features etc.

18. Don't introduce fake exposed floor joists or beams, either of synthetic materials made to look rather like timber, or wood ones which have been artificially and unconvincingly "distressed".

19. Don't paint exposed ceiling timbers (structural floor timbers) in that range of blackish "Tudoresque" preparations. This practice is rightly disliked by old buildings specialists to-day; although it was generally favoured in the 19th century and on into the 1950's. It is hell to get off, but repays the effort.

20. Don't use black paint on conventional softwood joists of open cottage ceilings. You are by inference suggesting that they are old hardwood beams.

21. Don't employ any of the odious "smoke-stained" plaster colours and finishes between joists which disfigure so many public houses.

22. Don't pug ceilings with sand to provide sound insulation, unless the joist and/or beam structure is robust enough to carry the considerable extra weight.

23. Don't forget to put hatches in plain top floor ceilings. Generous roof space access for work, inspections and storage is tremendously helpful.

24. Don't imagine that a naked display of repair work in the form of structural steel beams, stirrups and fish plates will always be acceptable by virtue of its "honesty".

Do's

CEILINGS AND CORNICES

1. Do ensure that original plaster ceiling mouldings, cornices etc. are carefully preserved in situ. This applies not only to mouldings in main rooms, but in bedrooms, kitchens and stair wells. Figs 40—97 inc.

2. Do avoid cutting across plasterwork decoration when dividing rooms in old houses. This will often mean that you cannot divide a room at all if the plasterwork is of any quality.

3. Do, if you have decided to divide a room which has timber or plaster cornices, make sure that you continue the mouldings along the new partition walls. This is an expensive nuisance, but it is **vital**.

4. Do try your best to repair and replace old ceiling mouldings where they are missing or damaged. This means research, ingenuity and very possibly specialist work. Simple details can sometimes be run or modelled by an amateur.

5. Do, if you are introducing **new** plasterwork in a traditional idiom (say, the Adam manner, or early 17th century strapwork) try to incorporate the date in the design. It is a great kindness to old buildings 'experts', who must otherwise assess such features on their style. Fig 52.

6. Do remove ugly, modern patterned and textured papers from ceilings. Also strip off unsuitable Victorian papers with raised designs, or compostion ornament, from earlier houses to which they have been added. **Note**: Attractive papier mâché ("paper stucco") ceiling designs of classical derivation were common by the end of the 18th century, so seek expert advice if unsure about what you might be removing.

7. Do use white emulsion paint for almost all plasterwork on ceilings. Of course this is not the medium which would have been employed in, say, the 18th century, and in an important house it is worth researching the types of paint which might originally have been used. (Also see pages 14, 15, 16.)

8. Do, if a coloured background **is** required to set off moulded details, exercise extreme caution in your choice of colour. Many colours look repellent in conjunction with old plasterwork. Neo-classical Adam-type ceilings may correctly have background colours in the pastel shades of blue or green, etc. used in the late 18th century.

9. Do, when exposing or stripping timber ceilings (boards, joists or beams) look out for traces of early painted decoration. It is rare and to be treasured if you are lucky enough to have it. In Britain, painted timber designs are normally no later than the beginning of the 17th century in domestic buildings.

10. Do leave any early exposed structural beams or joists in as natural a state as possible. This may mean stripping the wood of Victorian or modern paints or varnishes without damaging any mouldings or original decorative paintwork. The principle also applies to exposed roof trusses in barns, converted mills etc. and in the attics of houses, although those which post-date the mid-17thC. may often be painted with ordinary white emulsion to advantage.

11. Do look for carpenters' marks in the form of Roman numerals. They are usually incised on the principal rafters, collars and tie beams of trussed roofs in stone and brick houses. They are also found on all components of timber-framed buildings.

12. Do take care when repairing old roof timbers (especially those in hardwood with pegged joints) that you photograph the trusses, common rafters, wind braces and everything else of significance before you start. If you are inclined to believe the roof may be of architectural interest, obtain expert advice. It would be a shame to spoil or destroy a fine medieval crown post roof, for example.

13. Do, when repairing or altering rooms which must have exposed hardwood beams and joists, re-use old ones from your own building, or salvaged from elsewhere. Such ceilings will often be 17th century or earlier. However, in farmhouses and cottages they may be 18th century.

14. Do use square-edged softwood exposed joists for open ceilings in rough buildings. For these nothing looks better than white emulsion paint (Fig 97) although they may be left unpainted and unsealed in some cases.

15. Do, when painting old plasterwork, take care to avoid further reducing the definition of the detail. Some ceiling plaster, which has already been almost obliterated by successive layers of paint, may first need careful cleaning and restoration. The same goes for paint on finely moulded woodwork.

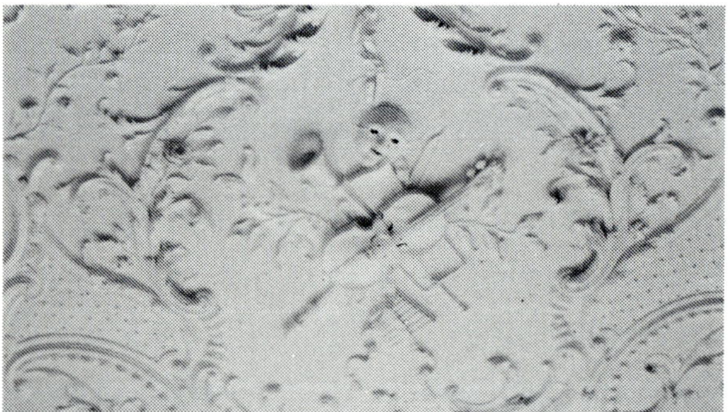

There are more genuinely Rococo ceilings in England than might be supposed, and this one, thought to have been carried out by Flemish craftsmen, is a very fine example from the 1730's. It epitomises all that is best in that lively and elegant style, with its crisp and inventine 'C' and 'S' scrolls and charming musical trophy. Much 18C plasterwork of high quality is rightly attributed to Italians; but there were numerous British masters capable of achieving these results.

1. Don't remove old and sometimes worn flagstones from floors. They are often one of a house's most attractive features — perhaps the **only** attractive feature.

2. Don't cover up old flagstones, bricks or quarry tiles. They are an asset to be cherished. If they are uneven, you can adjust the levels of the worst areas by lifting and introducing some weak mortar underneath.

3. Don't lay flagstones too far apart to "make them go further". It means having large unsightly areas of mortar in between.

4. Don't point up bricks, tiles and flagstones with mortar of unsuitable colour. A network of pale grey lines will spoil the whole effect.

5. Don't lay floors in crazy paving. They nearly always look like modern patios.

6. Don't cover old floors with acres of fitted carpet. Try to leave at least a polished surround upon which to stand furniture so that the room doesn't look stuffy.

7. Don't choose carpets with strong, modern patterns, or badly imitated old designs. They always look harsh and recent.

8. Don't in really old houses — 17th century and earlier — automatically go to the expense of levelling up the floor boards. It may be a part of the charm that a tennis ball put down at one end of the room will roll eerily to the other. It is a nuisance, but you will just have to chock up your furniture.

9. Don't choose floor finishes and patterns which are either too grand for a rough cottage, or not grand enough for a smooth house.

10. Don't allow smooth finish and easiness of cleaning to win over appearance of age, patina and character.

11. Don't lay any kind of patterned linoleum or similar material, without the greatest caution in your choice. Nearly all look wrong in old houses (i.e. pre-Victorian). See note on Georgian canvas coverings under No 17 in the Do's section.

12. Don't, as a rule, lay modern synthetic floor tiles in the more important rooms, halls or passages. Save them for laundries, bathrooms and lavatories, or occasionally kitchens. If you can afford alternatives, don't use them at all in earlier houses.

13. Don't strip out old floor boards which can reasonably be saved, especially if they are of oak or other hardwood. Early floor boards tend to be wide. Twelve inches was quite normal in the 17th century. If you find hardwood boards running the same way as the joists — and rebated into them, — look out, you probably have a Tudor or medieval floor.

14. Don't sand off the carefully built-up patina from old wood floors. This can be almost as bad as stripping two hundred years of built-up polish from a piece of Georgian furniture.

15. Don't paint floor boards in earlier houses (say before 1840). They may not look too bad that way if the damage is already done, but don't set the precedent yourself. Old floors decorated with painted designs are exceedingly rare, examples usually being 18th century.

16. Don't seal floors of any kind, old or new. Just use wax polish (see under Do's section).

17. Don't apply any kind of clear varnish-like material. It can kill the look of age on old floors, and prevents any improvement of new ones. Varnished floors also require regular patching.

18. Don't stain new boards or blocks in unsuitable modern shades which purport to echo period tones. At least experiment first. "Georgian mahogany" may look far from 18th century when it is down, and is impossible to eradicate.

19. Don't blithely nail down loose boards without checking for hidden wiring and pipework. Never secure floor boards with any kind of nail which cannot be punched below the surface.

An excellent method of obtaining a low cost natural slate floor is to cut old riven roofing slates to the desired size. They can then be laid on a thin levelling screed of mortar, which should be coloured to blend in, avoiding the pale grey tram-line effect between the rows. The pointing of the floor shown above is a bit too light.

FLOORS

1. Do make an effort to save, or reveal, old floors. These will include flagstones, tiles, bricks, boards, wood blocks and hardwood strip. Figs 105 — 114.

2. Do make it a general principle to retain or lay floors of natural materials, which have their own qualities of texture and colour. Unfortunately, many people's first reaction is to cover any existing stone, slate, brick or tile floor with, at worst, a mortar screed; or at best, acres of vinyl tiles or carpet of unsuitable design.

3. Do look out for rare and interesting floors, such as boards with painted designs (often 18th century), pebbles (sometimes in cross passages) Fig 106, medieval tiles, wide boards (rested in rebates parallel to and between the joists), inlaid or marquetry floors (usually 17th century but sometimes late 18th or early 19thC.).

4. Do, when excavating or re-laying solid ground floors, look out for rare examples of floors composed of animal bones, sometimes laid in patterns. These may be found in medieval houses. If possible they should be kept as found, but if this is totally impracticable, they should be photographed, and a panel left in any new finish through which a part can still be seen.

5. Do investigate the following hard floor finishes as suitable for use in old houses — marble flagstones, freestone flags (such as York stone paving), granite flagstones, slate flagstones (riven or sawn), clay quarry tiles, plain clay tiles, Spanish and Provençale tiles, bricks of good colour and texture. Polished concrete flagstones can also be surprisingly effective. Figs 105 — 119.

6. Do consider as a 'cottage' substitute for genuine flagstones, the use of cut-to-size roofing slates. They should be very carefully bedded in a mortar screed of toning colour.

7. Do realise that it is sometimes possible to lift and re-level a nice old brick or stone floor if it is really too uneven for safety. But think hard before doing so. Character of this kind is easily lost and you may break more that you bargained for.

8. Do preserve floors of patterned tiles, or those consisting of plain coloured tiles set in patterns, which you may find in Victorian and Edwardian houses. Original ones are usually in halls, passages and conservatories. Fig 116.

9. Do, where the floors of kitchens, laundries and similar rooms have had to be screeded, consider the use of a cork finish. This may be polished to advantage.

10. Do think of using terazzo as a finish for solid floors in laundries, kitchens and downstairs bathrooms. It is very easy to wash and is hard-wearing; but must be laid by specialists; and the colour and type of chippings well chosen.

11. Do investigate as wood floor possibilities:— hardwood t. & g. boards; softwood t. & g. boards; hardwood or softwood strip flooring; wood blocks; hardwood parquet; wood mosaic panels. Fig 118.

12. Do, as a general rule, wax polish all wood floors, leaving generous areas free of carpet, as this gives furniture a better setting and helps to enhance the atmosphere of an old house.

13. Do, if traditional methods appeal to you, try polishing new wood with a 3:8 parts mixture of beeswax and turpentine. Beeswax can still be bought in small cakes, and is rendered down in a double boiler with spirits of turpentine. Some colouring pigment may be added.

14. Do run stains into new softwood floorboards, and then seal with wax polish only. The stains should be very carefully selected for colour by experiment. The patina will develop in ratio to the frequency of polishing. Do therefore invest in the most sturdy electric floor polisher you can afford.

15. Do consider having a floor of natural wood boards (unstained or polished) which is kept clean by the dry scrubbing method. If you wish to follow the 18th century practice, you will first broadcast, and then brush up, damp sand to pick up fluff and dust. Then throw down sweet-smelling herbs, which are brushed hard into the surface of the boards to develop colour and scent. Finally you brush these up again. (This kind of thing is, of course, for fully paid-up enthusiasts). Fig 113.

16. Do think of the following carpets, rugs and mats for use in old houses, having due regard to the style and quality of the building.

    a) Hand-knotted Oriental rugs of all kinds (these are delectable in any setting). Chosen carefully, modern ones are excellent, but the old or antique are especially appealing.

    b) Flat woven Kelims and other folk rugs, like Indian Durries.

    c) Hand-made rag rugs (usually for cottages).

    d) Antique carpets of various kinds.

    e) Needlework carpets. (Vulnerable but intensely pleasing).

    f) Wilton broadloom in gentle colours, but be sparing.

    g) Haircords in neutral colours, heavy woven twills and similar plain but robust coverings.

    h) Sisal matting.

i) Hand-made stitched rugs of really good design.

j) Indian felt numdahs (suitable for bedrooms).

k) Rope mats (cottages etc).

l) Rush matting (preferably the cabled type rather than the square panels).

m) Sheepskins and other animal skins.

17. Do inspect anonymous rolls of canvas in cupboards or attics. You might just have some original 18th century painted floorcloth. It is also worth keeping an eye open for these under existing old carpets.

A fine parquetry floor in an early 19C house which is probably rather later than the building itself — perhaps c.1840. It has a delightful border with contrasted hardwood stringing, subtly designed to give the impression of being interlaced.

DOORS AND DOOR FURNITURE Don'ts

1. Don't take out original doors of the predominant period of a house, or later doors which fit in with a clearly established decorative phase in the building's history. **Note**: In some cases you may wish to return a building totally to its original, say, Tudor style. In others it may clearly be desirable to retain beautiful and interesting architectural schemes of later periods. In others again you may wish to expunge ugly Victorian aberrations.

2. Don't remove old door architraves, or overdoors, unless they are later additions which do not accord with the period style of the room.

3. Don't fit any form of modern flush door in an old house. This has a devastating visual effect in an old building.

4. Don't fit doors which are too grand for the style and period of a building. Some cottages may demand ledged, or ledged-and-braced plank doors, while others may reasonably have simple panelled ones. Study the period and flavour of the building.

5. Don't fit simple ledged doors in rooms which have any pretensions to architectural style or elegance, unless the building is sufficiently early in date to suggest that it would be correct.

6. Don't open up new doorways without ensuring that there is a visually respectable length of return wall to either side of the opening.

7. Don't assume that all new door openings should be made for doors of the modern standard size 2′9″ x 6′6″. Old doors were usually wider and heights varied greatly. You may need to have new doors specially made which are in keeping with the scale and proportion of the rooms.

8. Don't, as a general rule, fit any kind of door with clear glass panes arranged in such a way that they present an unresolved duality. The exception to this suggestion is the door which is meant to adhere to a consciously Victorian pattern in keeping with the house; or one which relates to an intended design of Continental derivation. The latter is sometimes demanded in an 18th century building. **Note**: Window panes, arranged in pairs create an unresolved duality. Place them in threes and the duality is resolved.

9. Don't fit, or retain, any door with obscured glass panes. This does not include some Victorian stained glass, or frosted or etched types which might appropriately be kept in later 19th or early 20th century buildings.

10. Don't strip formal panelled doors and leave them unpainted, unless they were clearly intended to be so in the first place. The fashion for stripped pine has meant that people have tended to expose every piece of timber in sight, regardless of period.

DOORS AND DOOR FURNITURE

11. Don't assume that absolutely all faked graining effects on old doors should be eliminated. You might just have an original from the late 17th century, or it could be a late Victorian door which is both correct and ugly.

12. Don't wallpaper the panels of doors.

13. Don't fit modern forms of door handle in old houses. This includes plastic and bakelite door knobs as well as plastic and aluminium lever handles, also steel types with bronze or sherardized finishes. Unsympathetic kinds of door furniture abound.

14. Don't fit imitation brass door furniture made of thinly coated steel etc, or put lacquer on real brass fittings. There is evidence to suggest that brass was sometimes lacquered in the 18th century; but it is nonetheless,an abhorrent practice.

15. Don't use Tudoresque wrought iron fittings for door handles, hinges and window fastenings. If the house is early enough to merit this kind of treatment (17th century or before) seek expert advice, or copy authentic examples of the period.

16. Don't use reproduction Adam or French ormolu door furniture, however faithfully copied, on doors of the wrong style and period. It may look fine in Osterley or the Musée Carnavalet, but decidedly bogus in a Queen Anne rectory.

17. Don't be tempted to fix the often pretty china finger plates to panelled doors in 18th century houses. Most of them are more suited to 19th century villas. Glass finger plates look modern and suggestive of the hotel suite.

The designers of Regency houses often employed the agreeable device of throwing two rooms into one by fitting big double doors. Another method of achieving the same effect was to hang a number of narrow panelled doors which could be folded back like a screen. This building, slightly post-dates the Regency; but is still typical.

DOORS AND DOOR FURNITURE

1. Do retain, and repair if necessary, any original doors you are lucky enough to have in your building.

2. Do research, in this and other books, the kind of doors, frames and architraves which are in keeping with the period of your house. Also look carefully at authentic examples. In buildings of the 17th century and earlier, pay great attention to any door arches, their shape, and any mouldings or spandrel decoration, etc.

3. Do salvage suitable old doors and door cases, for re-use in a house whenever the opportunity arises.

4. Do employ the services of a good joinery works to make properly detailed doors and door surrounds, which are in keeping with your house. If you get them right, nobody should need to touch them for another 200 years.

5. Do, as a general rule, use the following types of doors in these periods:—

   - 17th century and earlier — some were framed like wainscotting with vertical boards nailed to the framework; but most were ledged plank doors.
   - Late 17th and early 18th century — normally two panels, but sometimes a short one between two long ones, or a long one between two short ones. Also pairs of doors in similar patterns; and ledged doors in many cottages and lesser farmhouses.
   - Throughout the rest of the 18th century, the Regency and early Victorian periods — usually six panels; but ledged doors continued at a vernacular level.
   - Second half of the 19th century — four panels were often used. However, ledged types still continued in smaller and rougher dwellings; while framed doors with boards on one side were popular for utilitarian and institutional Victorian buildings.

   Note: This is a very rough guide and there are, of course, plenty of exceptions in most periods. For example, 8 panels were not at all unusual in the late 17th century, and a lot of houses had six-panel types in late Victorian times. (See Figs 120 — 165).

6. Do, if introducing or replacing ledged doors in early buildings, try first to obtain old hardwood boards which have a mature appearance. You can, of course, use new boards, and there are those who believe this is the only "honest" way.

7. Do remember that early door planks may have an adzed, finish. (See "Terms Explained"). If you can find somebody who really knows how to finish timber in this way, employ him, but don't distress the timber with badly faked finishes. Perhaps the best answer when finishing oak for doors in earlier houses is to hand plane the boards and ledges.

DOORS AND DOOR FURNITURE

8. Do try to use the correct method of fixing ledges to door planks. Traditionally these are joined with nails, driven through the timber, and clenched over. (Figs 123 & 133). In 17th century and earlier buildings they often had large stud heads, which were sometimes faceted. (Figs 130, 134 & 143). Some doors were of timber pegged construction.

9. Do think carefully before using any carved ornament when making doors and door frames. Unless you are able to get it absolutely right it can look spurious. A simple stopped chamfer of the right kind on the frame may be perfectly appropriate.

10. Do pay attention to the mouldings and details of door cases, especially of architraves and any panels to the jambs of the door opening. This usually applies in more formal houses of the late 17th, 18th and 19th centuries.

11. Do study the methods of hanging old doors in this book and elsewhere, so that you use the correct type of hinge for the period. Variations of the strap hinge will account for most doors of the 16th century and earlier, while types of 'H' and 'L' hinge will carry you on through much of the 17th and 18th centuries. All these types were nailed to the doors and frames, not screwed. Figs 131,143,145,153,and 166.

12. Do retain original hinges, locks, keys and handles of old doors and cupboards. Figs 141,166 and 167.

13. Do notice that early iron strap hinges were often sandwiched between the vertical planks and the framing members on the inner face of the door. This is clumsy, but correct. Figs 122 & 140.

14. Do sometimes use iron 'T' hinges with plain, lobed or sometimes spear shaped ends for late 16th and early 17th to mid 17th century doors. Study the detail carefully and ensure hand-forged finish.

15. Do use butterfly wrought-iron hinges on cupboard doors of 16th and 17th century vintage (Fig 166). The chamfered 'H' hinge, which may sometimes have shaped ends, is often suitable in the 17th century. The so-called "cock's head" elaboration of the 'H' hinge could also be considered for some 17th century work. (Fig 166)

16. Do remember that original wrought-iron strap hinges with curled back ends like hooks, anchors or fleur-de-lys are quite often medieval.

17. Do use butt hinges for panelled doors of mid to late 18th, and 19th century houses. Polished hardwood doors will probably require brass butts, perhaps with ball or turned ornamental ends to the pins.

DOORS AND DOOR FURNITURE

18. Do employ Norfolk or Suffolk thumb latches for ledged and braced cottage doors. These may be ironmonger's black japanned type (19th and 20th century) or some very straightforward wrought-iron design made up by your blacksmith at the forge. Fig 136, and below.

19. Do use plain iron or wood sneck latches for ledged doors. Also use hardwood or wrought iron bolts. Figs 123, 133, 134, 136, 137 and 139.

20. Do use iron latches with round ring or shaped drop-ring handles for early ledged doors (16th and 17th century). Fig 133. These may also be used for Victorian Gothic doors.

21. Do use brass lever handles of authentic design for some 18th and 19th century panelled doors, especially for those hung in pairs.

22. Do retain, or obtain, brass rim locks with knobs or drop loop handles for late 17th and 18th century doors in formal houses. Fig 167.

23. Do use plain ironmonger's stamped steel rim locks and latches for 19th century cottages, and fit brass or rather plain china knobs. Fig 167.

24. Do use brass, china or wooden knobs for panelled doors of 19th century houses. Also employ scaled down versions for pine or painted cupboards; and consider the revolving wooden 'button' or 'turnbuckle'. (See below).

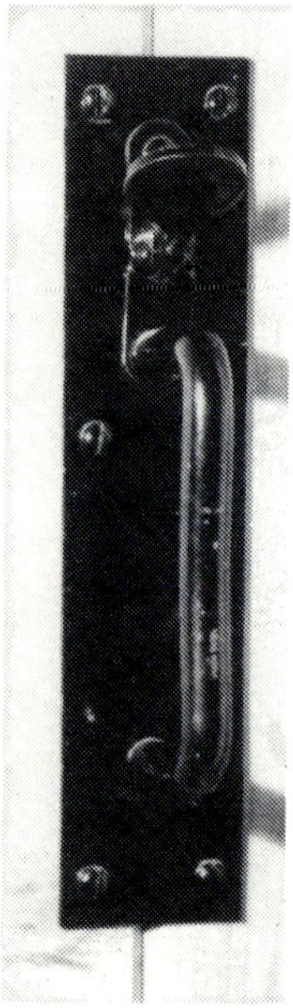

(Left) The practical and traditional black japanned thumb latch or Norfolk latch is still widely available. It is ideal for cottage doors, especially the ledged type. The thumb piece lifts the sneck which passes through a slot in the door. This, in turn, lifts the latch itself.

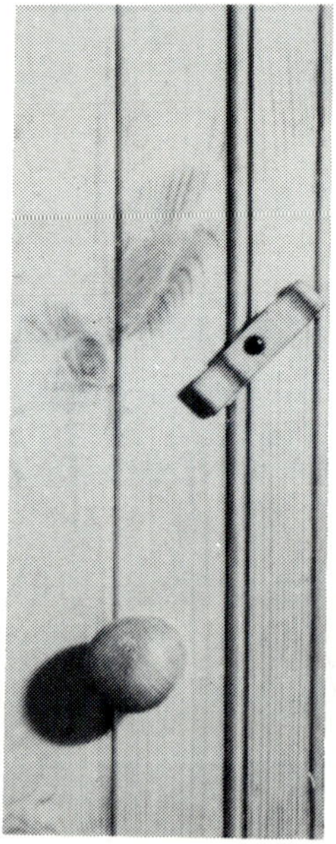

(Right) The plain wooden, or sometimes iron, "button" or "turnbuckle" is a suitable and traditional fitting for cupboard doors. Wooden knobs, like this one, are also in keeping. Brass knobs are another pleasant alternative and can be effective when used with secret touch latches. The latter do not show and the door opens or closes when you press it.

See Also Pattern Guide Fig. 167, p.82

1. Don't, above all, strip out old staircases, unless their condition is beyond redemption; or, in the case of rough cottages, the re-allocation of space makes it imperative. **Note**: In the latter case, you may be able to re-use the old stairs in a new position, but you should at least try to design any new stairs in the spirit of the building.

2. Don't confuse original staircases in their correct positions with later substitutes. These, if ugly or unsuitable, should be ruthlessly removed. It requires judgement, and sometimes advice.

3. Don't use modern staircase designs in old houses, as a general rule.

4. Don't use aggressively modern designs for new staircases in rough cottages. The simple softwood ladder type is an inoffensive possibility, but can sometimes strike a rather too contemporary note.

5. Don't fit modern spiral staircases, or copies of Victorian cast iron ones, in prominent positions in old houses. There are certain times when a simple spiral staircase may prove very useful, but it should not be obviously at variance with any clearly defined existing architectural theme.

6. Don't gratuitously devise split-level hall and living areas with shallow steps and balustrades. They tend to look like sets in television plays. Building Regulations sometimes make such steps and platforms imperative; but avoid them if you can.

7. Don't box in parts of staircases with modern materials, like plywood, hardboard, peg-board, chipboard, etc.

8. Don't tamper with the original mouldings and panelling associated with staircases and landings. Among these will often be panelling to handrail height (Fig 177) and console brackets under arches.

9. Don't alter the features of old staircases by replacing balusters, newels, handrails, etc. with others in unsuitable styles or materials.

10. Don't paint parts of staircases which should be in natural polished wood.

11. Don't, as so many people have over the years, decide that because a polished handrail, or similar feature, has been paint-splashed that it would be easier to paint the whole thing over. A great many fine finishes have been buried in this way.

12. Don't apply varnishes or polyurethane finishes to the natural wood surfaces of staircases.

13. Don't use stair-carpet on fine hardwood stair treads, as a general rule. If a stair-carpet is thought essential then see Do's No 8.

14. Don't lay fitted carpet across the entire width of the treads of more formal staircases in old houses. Leave a generous margin of polished or painted wood on either side, and perhaps employ attractive brass stair rods.

15. Don't fail to remove ugly Victorian stained or frosted glass from 18th or early 19th century staircase windows. It is no visual consolation to say that they form part of the history of the house. Save them intact for somebody with a building of the right period. Remember, however, that there is such a thing as Georgian painted glass decoration, so be careful.

16. Don't paint cast or wrought iron balustrades in "the colours of your choice". They should normally be either black or white, and there are those who would recommend black only. Personally, I prefer flat paint for these, but it is arguable. Gold embellishment should be discreetly applied in gold-leaf, not paint. This does not mean that owners in former times always showed similar discretion.

A superbly graceful geometric staircase which is typical of the first quarter of the 19C. This style however, was still a favourite in the period 1825 to c.1840. Note the charming curved dog gate with its brass top rail and knob finials. The pattern of the balustrade is almost identical to that in Fig. 194. It makes an interesting comparison between the merits of using white or black paint for this kind of ironwork. Readers will see that both work well; and that location and personal preference will play a large part in your choice.

STAIRCASES

1. Do find out whether the staircase of an old house or cottage is original to the building; is an old, but later addition or something recently concocted.

2. Do replace a staircase which is out of keeping with the period of a building, and either seek specialist advice, or design something yourself which genuinely accords with the rest of the house. This does not mean that you should rip out a fine Georgian staircase from a 17th century house which has been modernised in, say 1760.

3. Do remember that old staircases often conform to a different plan during different periods, i.e. a newel stair in a medieval house (Fig 168) or a small open well of short flights in a 17th century one. Fig 178.

4. Do note the distinction between country staircases and those in fashionable towns of importance. In the latter, balusters, for instance, may be of the same pattern, but very much more spindly than those in a rural farmhouse.

5. Do consider, for cottages, the traditional staircase with winder steps. This type is often entirely enclosed with a boarded partition, and is shut off at the top or bottom with a simple door. A light handrail is fixed to the wall.

6. Do try to use a handrail of a correct design for the period. This requires research into materials, cross-sections and possibly local practices. The same care applies to other details like balusters, newel posts, etc.

7. Do take pains to finish the natural wood of staircase components with suitable stains and/or polishes, ensuring a good mellow colour and a pleasant waxed finish. In some cases hardwoods may be left without treatment of any kind to adopt their own colour and patina. Especially in late 18th and 19th century houses, a polished hardwood (usually mahogany) handrail may be used in conjunction with white painted newels and balusters. Fig 196, 197.

8. Do, if you must carpet the stairs, use very plain haircord in some fairly neutral colour, or perhaps a strip of Wilton and always leave a border of bare wood on either side. Oriental knotted runners can also look well, but they are expensive. The traditional Turkeys or Afghans in blues and reds are effective.

9. Do, in the case of polished hardwood flights of steps, consider using some very inconspicuous form of tread pad. Polished treads can be fairly dangerous, but it must be admitted that they look much better left completely bare.

10. Do, if designing a new staircase for an old house, be aware that it must meet the requirements of the Building Regulations. There are instances, especially in small cottages, where the Building Regulations could make the right kind of staircase impossible. Seek a relaxation of the regulations if necessary.

11. Do realise that buildings with public uses, such as hotels and offices should conform with the Fire Precautions Act. This could mean that a staircase must be ruined by being encased, and the landing disfigured with hideous fire doors.

12. Do appreciate that it is YOUR responsibility to AVOID trying to use an old house for purposes which must inevitably make it subject to the kind of changes outlined in No 11 above. If the building is listed, no responsible local authority for their part, should allow a change of use which makes it necessary to ruin the character of the interior.

* * * * *

Original scenic wallpapers like this grisaille dated 1824, are of exceptional interest, quite apart from their obvious merits from the decorative point of view. The example shown is by the French designer, Mader père, and was printed by the Paris firm, Dufour et Leroy, using six blocks on small sheets measuring 21¾ins x 17¼ins. It depicts a typically neo-classical theme:— 'Les Jeux Olympiques'. The owners of the house made sure that it was expertly restored and its origins researched.

1. Don't tear out old fireplaces, or parts of them, like pilasters, architraves, shelves or pediments unless (for instance), they are ugly Victorian replacements in an 18th century room.

2. Don't block up old flues which are no longer needed until you are quite sure where they lead, and whether or not they may be made to serve some other purpose — to contain new pipework or heat ducts, for example.

3. Don't change the scale and proportion of an **old** fireplace opening, as a general rule.

4. Don't make new fireplaces which do not respect the proportions of an old room, its period and general character. Avoid low, horizontal shapes such as the modern ensemble which gathers a small fire opening, log recess and area of blank stone or brick wall under a long shelf. There are numerous ready-made fireplaces available and hardly any of them could be contemplated for an old building.

5. Don't introduce modern grates into old fireplace openings.

6. Don't insert fitted electric fires or modern gas appliances into old fireplace openings, as a general rule. Gas fires began in the 1870's and electric ones of drole design in the Edwardian era. Clearly, flat dwellers in Victorian town houses will often need gas or electric fires. Use good judgement.

7. Don't use modern iron fire baskets of spuriously medieval design in old fireplaces, such as the fleur-de-lys encrusted excesses of the ready-made ironwork firms. There **were** early baskets somewhat like these, but modern versions tend to look surburban, rather than genuinely 16th century.

8. Don't, as a matter of course, point fireplace walls or chimney-breasts in cottages leaving the stonework or brickwork exposed. This practice is by no means always successful — especially in 18th and 19th century buildings. The lintel and the jambs of the opening usually provide quite enough exposed texture, even in a rough cottage.

9. Don't use ugly forms of pointing in association with fireplaces of early buildings. Abide by the general principles for walls (see No 15 page 23).

10. Don't treat exposed stonework associated with an old fireplace wall with any kind of varnish or clear sealer. It will detract from its visual texture. If you are worried about dust or grit, then exposed stone is not for you.

11. Don't introduce fireplaces surrounded by vertical crazy paving stonework. They fail to please. There are many truly awful materials for surrounding a modern grate — some genuine and others sythentic. There is no need to employ any of them in an old house.

12. Don't buy modern reproduction 18th century fireplaces which are pseudo in their design and detailing, or do not relate to the period of the room. For example, avoid an Adam-style fireplace in either a room of 1830, or one of 1730.

13. Don't insert new lintels, in unsympathetic materials, over old fireplaces.

14. Don't be tempted to fit a mantelpiece or similar shelf above an early fireplace which should not have one. For example, above a plain, flat 16th century opening with a Tudor stone arch lintel, like that in Fig 208. It could mean either having to fix the shelf to the lintel itself and thus cutting it visually in two, or placing it high above, where the lintel stone finishes. There is no golden rule, and shelves are certainly very useful; but be careful.

15. Don't apply dark bituminous looking paints or stains to wooden fireplace lintels, already in situ. Rather try to remove the gunge from those already so treated.

16. Don't remove old iron bars, pot hooks, chimney cranes, or other interesting pieces of fireplace machinery, unless absolutely necessary. Fig 224.

17. Don't assume that bedroom fireplaces are "de trop" in modern Britain, and therefore block them up as a matter of course. They often form an important architectural feature. Anyway what can be more comforting than to lie in bed and watch the shadows from an open fire, flickering across the ceiling?

18. Don't insert modern slow burning stoves, and similar free-standing appliances, in old fireplaces without taking infinite care in your choice of design. There are some lovely ones available; but many can only be described as clumsy or even grotesque.

19. Don't, as a general rule, fit beaten copper hoods over down-hearths or dog grates. They usually look unconvincing. They may well be suitable for something art nouveau, however.

NOTE: There are few open fireplaces which do not smoke on occasions — usually the most inconvenient ones. Some smoke most of the time. No feeling owner will let this deter him from having one. Remedial measures can often be effective.

1. Do appreciate the value of an old open fireplace in any room. Correctly repaired or restored, it can be the most important factor as far as character, atmosphere and period are concerned.

2. Do rip out modern, ugly or unsuitable fireplaces and grates from rooms which are clearly intended to have something better.

3. Do ensure that you are not endangering the structure of an old fireplace in the process of removing a modern grate. It may need temporary support to a damaged lintel, chimney bar or brick arch.

4. Do provide a fireplace which is of the correct period or character for the age and architectural style of the room. All 18th century fireplaces are **not** either Adam or Louis Quinze.

5. Do study the examples in this book and elsewhere, when designing new fireplace surrounds in the classical manner. It is important that they conform to the basic trends of the period you are seeking.

6. Do use a grate of the correct style for the period of the fireplace. (See Pattern Guide and Terms Explained.)

7. Do repair and replace mouldings or other details of period fireplaces, even if they are late ones — 1890 for example. They all matter.

8. Do remember to treat continued chimneypieces (Figs 234, 235) as a visual whole, both decoratively and in any repairs or replacements.

9. Do look for evidence of old fireplaces which may have been blocked up or hidden behind later plaster finishes or linings. Also look at the outside of a building and trace chimneys to their appropriate fireplaces inside.

10. Do exercise great care when searching out old fireplace openings to avoid damaging original features, such as stone mouldings, old concealed tiles, carvings, grates, cloam ovens and hearth furniture. You would kick yourself if you accidentally broke up a valuable set of 17th century blue and white tiles, for example.

11. Do look for evidence of and retain any old fireplace furniture — chimney cranes, fire spit fittings, ovens, pot hooks, cast firebacks, niches, shelves or seats.

12. Do, if the house is an early one, call in expert advice before attacking what may be a unique fireplace in a decoratively or structurally frail condition. Some suggested sources of advice:— county rescue archaeologists, architectural historians, specialist architects, knowledgeable museum staff, and expert members of conservation groups.

13. Do trace the outlines of timber or stone fireplace lintels to determine the original size of the fireplace opening. Chip off trial patches of plaster, and tap walls to reveal concealed cavities.

14. Do leave the jamb stones and lintels of open hearths in unsophisticated buildings exposed, but pay great attention to the pointing. This should be kept well back from the face of the stones, and should be of toning colour and texture. Fig 207.

15. Do remember that some types of fireplace, especially those which have a large stone lintel as an essential feature, tend to look better without a mantelshelf. Some 17th century chimneypieces with heavy bolection moulding architraves should definitely **not** have mantelshelves. Sometimes these have been added at a later date, and may need to be removed. Fig 227 has no shelf; and Fig 228 has one. Both are in their original form.

16. Do use simple, wooden mantelshelves on shaped timber brackets over kitchen or cottage parlour fireplaces (usually 19th century). Fig 223.

17. Do consider lining inside splays of a late 17th or early 18th century fireplace openings with plain or blue and white tiles, preferably of the old Delft patterns. Similarly, employ Victorian patterned tiles (there are now some good designs on the market) for 19th century grates which demand them.

18. Do use marble or slate slips around the openings of classically derived chimneypieces (see Parts of a Room). Also use matching hearthstones.

19. Do consider purchasing a suitable oil painting to fill the specially provided wooden panel over an 18th century fireplace. (Fig 236) Late 17th century ones were often painted directly onto the panel by itinerant Dutch and Flemish topographical artists, Fig 229.

20. Do buy old cast-iron firebacks for open hearth fires. Alternatively, choose from among the many excellent modern reproductions. These are cast from old patterns, and are indistinguishable from the originals to any but the most expert observer. The fireback protects the wall structure at the back of the hearth, reflects heat into the room, as well as being decorative and helping to establish the desired period. Figs 254, 255.

21. Do use fire dogs to support the logs in a down-hearth. Design your own, by all means, and get the blacksmith to make them up from your sketches. Fig 256. Make sure they are robust and interesting, without being disagreeably folksey.

22. Do research and then sketch suitable fire baskets to be made up by your local blacksmith. Ready-made fire baskets are frequently of poor and unconvincing design. Exceptions to this are the excellent polished steel reproductions of original 18th century "dog grates". Fig 258, 259, 261.

23. Do use very plain and functional steel hoods for down-hearths or earlier forms of basket grates. Also consider a mellow brick hood, or one contrived from a lightweight reinforced plaster. Designs for this kind of thing require taste and a feeling for old houses. Many look very harsh and pseudo, even when made of genuine materials. Simplicity is the watchword, plus a regard for the age of the building and the natural materials used in its construction.

24. Do use smoke shutters in polished or stove-blacked steel, or in heat-resistant glass to lower the smoke line of fireplace openings, when necessary.

25. Do employ steel or brass club fenders (a Victorian invention) in front of suitable fireplaces. They are exceedingly practical and very decorative, whether old or good modern reproductions. They may be used in front of many 18th century fireplaces with impunity, and for a good number of other kinds as well. 18th century cut-steel fenders normally fitted across the fireplace opening itself, rather than standing out from it on the hearth stone.

26. Do use wood-burning or general purpose stoves in less sophisticated rooms, but have a care in your choice of design. Some look very modern and unpleasing.

Cast-Iron Grates and Firebacks

Since foundries continued to cast grates from patterns which had long ceased to be postively fashionable, the dates given here may be treated as a reasonably sound guide to period, without being definitive.

Some, like the dancing horseshoe example in Fig 248 and 282, actually bear the all important Class I registration mark for metal objects, which was used to protect manufacturers' designs from 1842 to 1883.

However, this is not quite the answer to prayer which it might at first seem. Marks on the backs of grates have frequently been made illegible by rust and wear.

The best marks may be found in the firebricks bolted around the sides and back of the firebasket; but there is no guarantee that they are original to the grate, unless they bear the same pattern or model number as the ironwork. Registration numbers replaced the diamond shaped mark in 1884.

Many grates, which could hardly fail to fit into the registration mark period were either not registered, or the foundries were not meticulous about putting the marks on their wares.

Cast firebacks, dog grates, brand irons and andirons, are all perfectly adapted to modern reproduction. It takes a very expert eye indeed to know the old from the new, since the design and materials are almost identical, whether the object was cast in 1680 or 1980.

Considerations of sentiment and antique value apart, there is no good reason why you should not use a grate or dogs of suitable and authentic design, even if they were made last week. Poor and flimsy fakes are, of course, repugnant.

Pattern Guide

The pictures which follow are principally intended as a pattern guide for those who wish to identify or re-create period features.

Although most examples are, indeed, of their period there are many types of design and construction which are common to more than one century. This is particularly so of doors and door furniture, for example.

Locks were rare assets in the late 15th and 16th centuries; and in country areas, were never easy or cheap to replace, until large scale manufacture began in the 18th century.

This meant that they would be fitted and re-fitted to one door after another. A sure sign of this is when the keyhole is the wrong way up; for rim and stock locks have to be either "left" or "right-handed", and are ordered accordingly.

The earliest form of hinge consisted of stout pins extending upwards and downwards from the top and bottom of the door. These pins fitted into the head and threshold of the doorway. However, the earliest type of hinge you will normally encounter, is the "strap" or "cross garnet". It is hung on a gudgeon pin which is spiked to the frame, or plug-fixed to the jamb stones. Variations of this basic method have been used for hundreds of years and are in general use for outbuildings to-day. Dating can only be done by assessing the finer points of pattern, decoration and workmanship.

As with most other features of old buildings, fireplaces become increasingly enigmatic about their origins as they get older and plainer. This is one of the prime difficulties in dealing with vernacular buildings.

In a palatial mansion, with any luck at all, you will see fireplace surrounds which incorporate many of the tell-tale mannerisms of their period. The grander and more up-to-the-minute a chimneypiece is, the easier becomes the task of slotting it into its appropriate quarter or third of a century.

In cottages and very simple houses, there may be almost no detail for you to date. Two granite posts and a lintel rudimentarily chamfered around the opening, could well be late 16th or early 17th century. But without some other features with which to cross-check the probabilities; together with some structural detective work, nobody can be certain.

What you **can** always do, is say: "If this part of the building is about the age I think it is, that is the sort of fireplace I'd expect to find in it."

Staircases do follow definite stylistic trends and forms of plan and construction. All the same, allowances must be made for the numerous exceptions which are either ahead of or behind the times. It should be remembered that owners had a way of fitting old staircases in new houses and vice-versa. Also, beware the meticulous Victorian fake!

Ceilings (fakes and copies apart) follow fairly clearly defined patterns, during different eras. But do not be over influenced by detail. Take good account of the overall effect, the weight, the flavour.

As soon as Renaissance ideas began to find their way into even the remoter areas of Britain in the 16th century, certain classical motifs started to appear in interiors. At first, they tended to be used in panelling and chimneypieces, but by the mid-17th century, they were common in ceilings too. From then on, you should not attach excessive importance to the use of a guilloche or a key pattern, for instance, as lone pieces of evidence for dating.

Pattern Guide

From the point of view of styling, in accordance with a building's predominant period, you should look for something typical and note the finer points of fixing, workmanship and design. Your next move should be to adapt it to your own purposes, without being too trite, twee, slavish or bombastic. This may involve using the pictures in this pattern guide as the starting point for further researches.

Dates of Kings and Queens — 1066 to 1952

Norman

William I	1066
William II	1087
Henry I	1100
Stephen	1135

Plantagenet

Henry II	1154
Richard I	1189
John	1199
Henry III	1216
Edward I	1272
Edward II	1307
Edward III	1327
Richard II	1377

Lancaster

Henry IV	1399
Henry V	1413
Henry VI	1422

York

Edward IV	1461
Edward V	1483
Richard III	1483

Tudor

Henry VII	1485
Henry VIII	1509
Edward VI	1547
Mary	1553
Elizabeth	1558

Stuart

James I	1603
Charles I	1625
Commonwealth	1649
Charles II	1660
James II	1685
William & Mary	1689
Anne	1702

Hanover

George I	1714
George II	1727
George III	1760
The Regency	1811
George IV	1820
William IV	1830
Victoria	1837

Saxe-Coburg

Edward VII	1901
George V	1910

Windsor from 1917

Edward VIII	1936
George VI	1936
Elizabeth II	1952

WALLS AND WINDOWS

2.

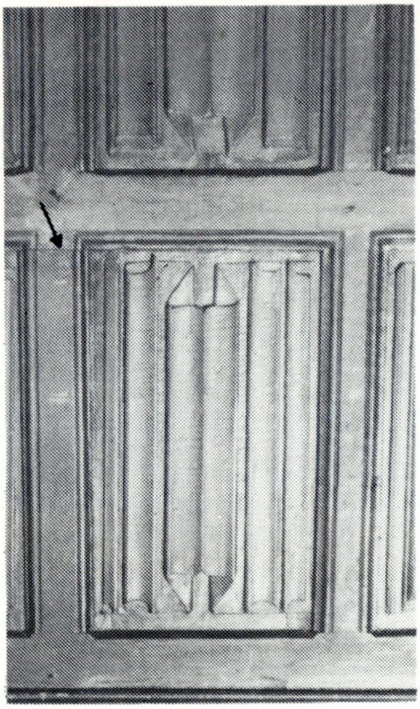

1. *Late 15C. oak linenfold panelling. Note the mason's mitre joint (indicated by the arrow). The stiles and rails are secured with pegs, and have simple stuck mouldings, omitted at the foot of each panel.*

2. *Late 15C. plank and stud partition, with deeply moulded head plate, matching the beams which are jointed to it. The studs have been bored with holes to the left, and are slotted to the right (not visible in picture) to allow the willow cross staves of wattle panels to be sprung into position. These would have been clay daubed. The studs have themselves been hacked as a key for plaster at some time.*

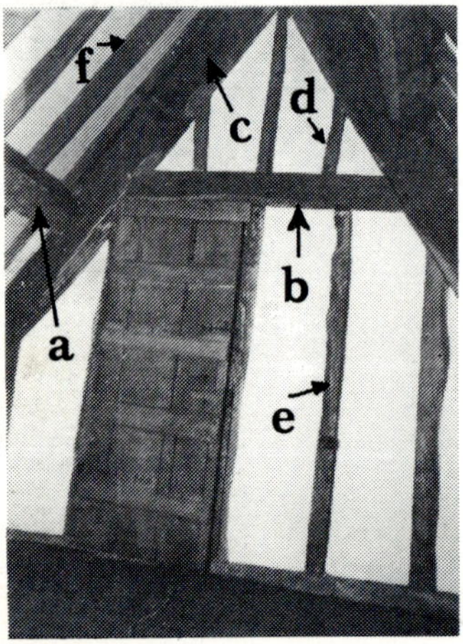

3.

3. *Late 16C. oak stud partition framed between the principal rafters and the collar of a roof truss with through purlins.*

a. Purlin
b. Collar
c. Principal rafter
d. Strut
e. Stud
f. Common rafter

4. *Late 16C. decorative oak carving set in a modern timber surround. The bands linking the rosettes, with their studs and lozenges suggest strapwork.*

4.

WALLS AND WINDOWS

5.

5. *Oak panelling, probably of late 16C. or early 17C. origin. The fluted or channelled design of the stiles suggests a Renaissance influence. A ball motif is seen above the rounded top of each flute — very reminiscent of the "scoop" pattern used on furniture of the period. The rails are scribed over the muntins. The panels have ovolo mouldings at top and sides.*

6. *Jacobean oak panelling c.1612. Note this early use of an architectural order (Ionic). The architrave running across the caps of the fluted and cabled pilasters, has been correctly sub-divided into fascias; but the frieze has a floral trail with heraldic shields in the Gothic spirit. The upper panels are arcaded and typical of the period.*

7.

7. *Early 17C. window with hollow chamfered granite mullion and panelled soffit above. The lead cames in which the diamond panes of the casement and fixed light are set, are tied to iron saddle-bars to give rigidity, in the traditional way.*

8.

8. *This window jamb panelling at the National Trust's Lanyhdrock House, dates from the 1630's. Note the fluted and cabled Corinthian pilasters and the floral arabesques on the pedestal. The geometric arrangement of the panel mouldings is typical of the early 17C.*

9. *Last quarter of 17C. The chimneypiece panelling with its swagged carving of leaves and berries (olive, laurel or bay) could equally date from the mid 17C. The Corinthian order used for the entablature is now well understood. Note the dentils have been omitted from the cornice, and that there is bead-and-reel enrichment on the architrave.*

10.

11.

10. *This late 17C. oak window with ovolo mullions has been revealed during building work. It is set in a timber framed wall and has been covered with lath and plaster on the outside. Note the original rectangular panes of very thin glass in lead cames, tied back to vertical timber bars. The adjoining doorway of the same period shows some of the covering laths against the light. Discreditably, this window was removed from a listed building and had to be put in a museum.*

11. *Typical late 17C. panelling, fielded and raised above the surrounding framework of rails, stiles and muntins. A bold bolection moulding runs around each panel; and the chair rail stops well short of the door case.*

12. *Close up of late 17C oak panelling. The chair rail, with it's firm torus moulding is characteristic.*

12.

13. *Mid to late 17C. form of muntin-and-plank partition. The planks are bevelled to slot into the muntins, which are decorated with very simple half inch stuck mouldings. Compare with 15C. version,* **2** *above.*

14. *Late 17C. raised panelling surrounded with bolection mouldings. The paper on the panels is modern.*

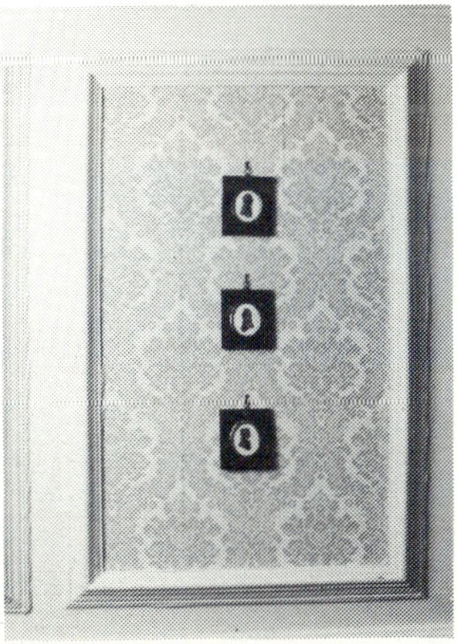

14.

15. *This casement with it's rectangular leaded lights is part of a cruciform window of timber pegged construction. Note the original hinges, with gudgeon pins spiked into the frame. The window is now positioned inside a passage with a later exterior wall in front it. It's style and construction suggest mid to late 17C. date.*

16. *Typical late 17C. panelling with bolection mouldings. The entablature is more or less Tuscan, and has a pulvinated frieze, characteristic of the period.*

16.

WALLS AND WINDOWS

17.

17. *Late 17C. original sash window with 40 panes of crown glass, some inscribed with dates or initials, probably done with a diamond ring. The glazing bars are very shallow from front to back. They are 1¼ inches wide, with an absolutely plain torus moulding to the inside. These mouldings were sometimes planted onto plain, shallow, T- section glazing bars.*

18. *Late 17C. panelling of characteristic pattern. The panelled pilasters of the chimneypiece are frequently seen at this time. Panels are bolection moulded, and in this case, the chair rail has been omitted. Note the panel over the fireplace, and also see 229.*

18.

19.

19. *Late 17C. or early 18C. pine fielded panelling in a small town house bedroom. Here, the dado has plain boards instead of containing panels to match those above the torus moulded chair rail. The muntins and rails have very simple stuck ovolo mouldings.*

20. *Skirting-board of wall in* **19.** *Typically, it is only about six inches high, and is moulded with a torus, cavetto and ogee.*

20.

21.

21. *Queen Anne panelling of the early 1700's. The panels are now sunk below the surface of the framing members, which can be moulded with a shallow ovolo or ogee. The chair rail consists of a 1¼ inch ledge, with a fillet on face, supported by a cyma reversa.*

22. *This fielded panelling is in a room which suggests a date somewhere in the second quarter of the 18C. There is no chair rail and the skirting has cavetto and ovolo mouldings, separated by a narrow fillet.*

22.

23. *The walls of this grand town house of the 1730's are no longer panelled, but plastered and decorated in the Palladian manner with lively applied ornament. This characteristic panel with shouldered corners, is surmounted by an eagle holding swags — a favourite device.*

24. *1730's stucco ornament consisting of a grotesque mask framed in 'S' scrolls, supporting swagged drapery. Below is a Vitruvian scroll.*

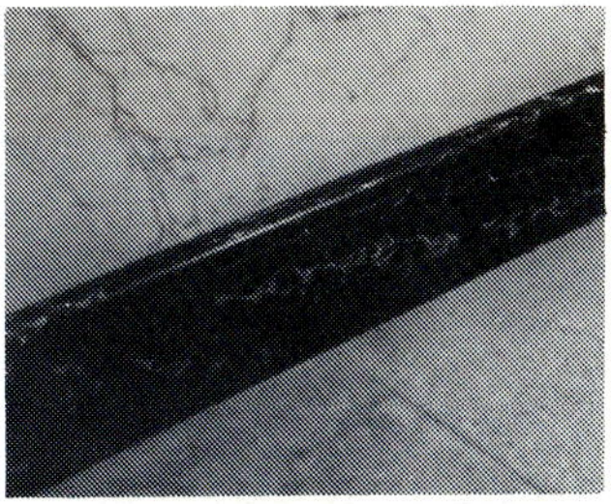

26. *Marbling (faux marbre) at Bath Preservation Trust's No.1 Royal Crescent has been carried out in paints, using feather brushes and twigs.*

25. *This sunk panelling in a house of c.1770 by John Wood the Younger, is carried out in plaster above the chair rail, and in timber below it. Note the egg and dart enrichment of the ovolo panel mouldings. The chair rail is a miniature classical cornice.*

25.

27. *Early 19C. applied mouldings in the hall of a Queen Anne house. Note the plain plaster dado, and the chair rail consisting of a flat band between mouldings. The architrave of the door on the right of the picture is absolutely typical of the period c.1810, with its corner blocks and roundels.*

27.

WALLS AND WINDOWS

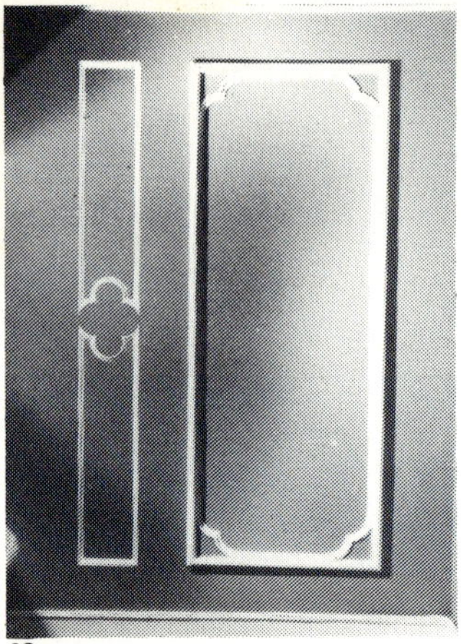

28.

28. *This Gothic plaster decoration is thought to date from the early 19C. With its quatrefoil in one panel and cusped corners in the other, it would be typical enough. The smaller panel has quadrant mouldings. The bigger one is surrounded by a heavy roll moulding outside a cavetto.*

29. *Victorian Louis XVI boiserie in the 19C. wing of a 17C. house. The tall panel beside the door is typically French in outline. The joists are exposed and moulded in what might be called château-style.*

30. *Victorian carved linenfold — rather lifeless and mechanical when compared with* **1**. *All the same it needs a very skilled craftsman to produce it.*

30.

29.

31. *Typical Art Nouveau embossed paper of the late 19C. or early 20C. in the dado of an 1840's house.*

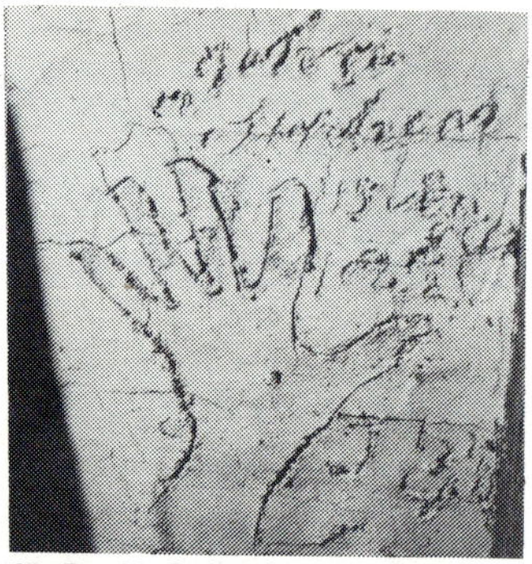

32. *The kind of evidence we always hope to find and seldom do. A workman has outlined his hand on the torching plaster inside the roof of a 19C farmhouse. The inscription reads: John Hopham, 15th. Jun, 1842. The rest is illegible.*

33.

34.

35.

36.

37.

38.

39.

33. *Stonework of interior walls should NOT be left exposed. It is not an authentic practice. However, this pointing is good. The mortar, if a little dark, has been kept back from the edges of the granite, and brushed to give texture. (Cottage: first half 19C).*

34. *The whitewashed look is one of the most successful ways of treating stone cottage walls, and sometimes brick to. The stones are visually muffled, but still retain their general outline.*

35. *This niche has been introduced later than the surrounding late 17C. panelling. The panelled pilasters have a Gothic flavour, which suggests the first Gothic revival of Strawberry Hill vintage (c.1750's). The chair rail has been cut back.*

36. *In the same late 17C. room as* **35**. *Here, the panel boards have been removed to allow a shelved recess and the original bolection mouldings remain.*

37. *Cupboard in a late 17C. room. The device of placing these and fireplaces in corners is typical of the period.*

38. *Early 19C. cupboard with diamond shaped decoration on the blocks above the moulded pilaster panels.*

39. *Regency Gothic glazing in the doors of this niche of c.1813. Note the unpanelled dado.*

40.

40. Last quarter 15C. This fine ceiling has richly carved intersecting oak beams with typically decisive mouldings. Note the grape vine trail on the soffits, and the gothic flavour of the carved boss. The joists too are decorated with torus and cavetto mouldings.

41. This Tudor ceiling of the late 15C. has moulded beams and heavy bosses at the intersections. The diagonal ribs in the panels suggest stone vault tracery. Short, wide boards span between beams.

42.

42. The deep chamfers of this massive early 16C oak beam are typical. The spade-like stops are less distinctive. The ceiling boards are modern.

43. A 16C. oak ceiling of stop-chamfered oak beams and joists.

43.

44.

44. *These intersecting oak beams in a 16C. manor-house are chamfered and plainly stopped. Iron angle plates have been used for repair.*

45. *A typical ribbed plaster ceiling of the 1570's with "turned" mouldings on the pendants. The flavour of the ornament is Gothic, the original workmanship was probably Italian; but this great hall was restored in the Mid 19C. (Trerice, National Trust).*

45a. *The kind of light, ribbed mouldings, with stylised paterae and leaves concealing the intersections, which were commonly used in the late 16C. (National Trust, Trerice).*

46. *Chamfered oak beams with stops — second half of 16C.*

CEILINGS AND CORNICES

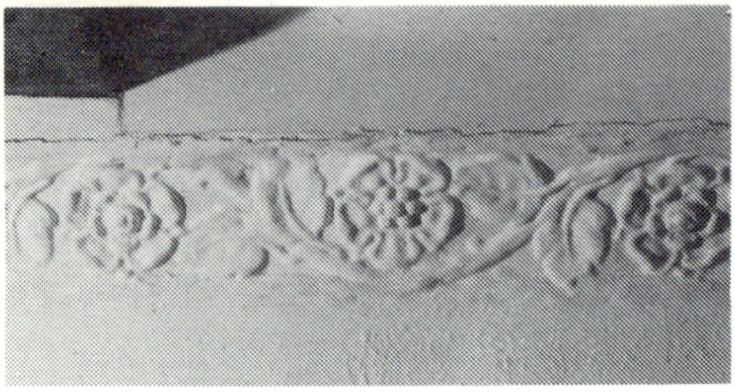

47. *Plaster cove with running ornament of leaves and rosettes in what may have been a minstrel's gallery. This is possibly early 16C., but could be much later. Trails of this kind were still being used in the 17C.*

47.

48. *Typical Elizabethan frieze (1572) in the Great Hall of the National Trust's Trerice. Classical influences are now at work. There is a more or less Doric cornice. The frieze motifs of sheaved and scrolled plant tendrils are symmetrically arranged, while the head in an oval frame recalls Romayne work. However, the classical orders are still transitional — bridging the gap between Gothic and Renaissance.*

49. *Also from Trerice, is this late 16C. plaster frieze, displaying shields, plant motifs and heraldic beasts — again typical of the period.*

50. *16C. form of frieze containing the usual kind of repeating plant ornament (Trerice).*

51.

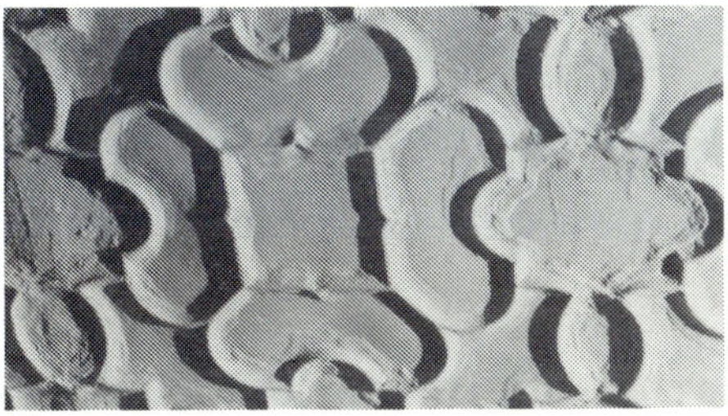

52.

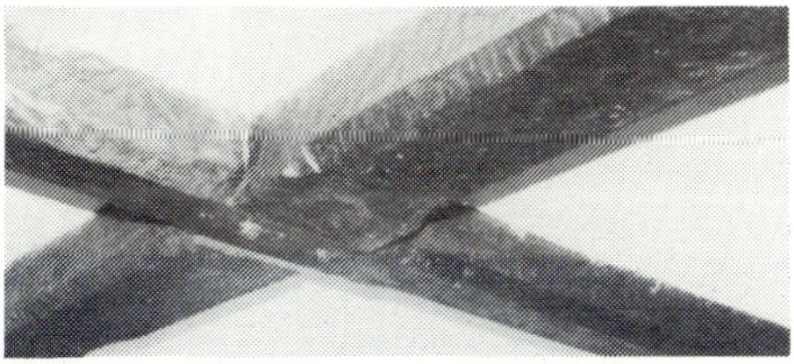

53.

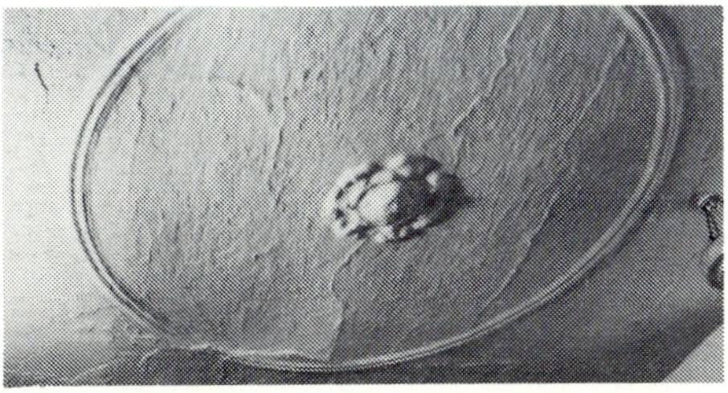

54.

51. *Quintessentially "Jacobean" in design, this barrel-shaped ceiling in the gallery of the National Trust's Lanhydrock dates from the 1630's. Note the flat, heavy bands which outline panels containing heraldic creatures and scenes from the Old Testament. Pendants are still in use, and to either side of the coat of arms, are typical examples of strapwork.*

52. *Although this example is likely to be mid-17C., the ribbed design of the ceiling has a distinctly 16C. flavour. A "finger and thumb" hand modelling technique is thought to have been used in part of its construction.*

53. *These oak beams with their relatively small stopped chamfers are possibly early 17C. They have been hacked all over at some later date to provide a key for plaster. The bolt heads denote modern repair work.*

54. *This farmhouse ceiling with its whitewash encrusted "Tudor" rose device is thought to date from the early 17C. It is just the sort of unassuming and slightly mysterious plasterwork which should be saved.*

CEILINGS AND CORNICES

55. *A continous trail of fruit and flowers decorates this bold and highly stylised frieze of the 1630's. The cornice moulding above is minimal.*

56. *Carved oak frieze in the panelled gallery of the National Trust's Lanhydrock. Although of the 1630's, the fondness for heraldic beasts and shields continues (see also* **49***).*

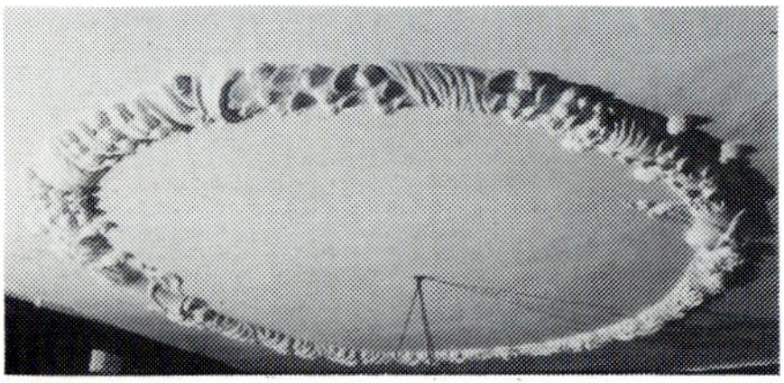

57. *Typical heavy plaster ceiling moulding of the second half of 17C. The tightly packed bay leaf garland bound with a wide ribbon, also incorporates elongated manneristic human figures and grotesque masks.*

58. *Detail from* **57***. Although grotesque masks are characteristic of the Renaissance, and this one is set in a Baroque scroll, it has a touch of the Gothic gargoyle about it.*

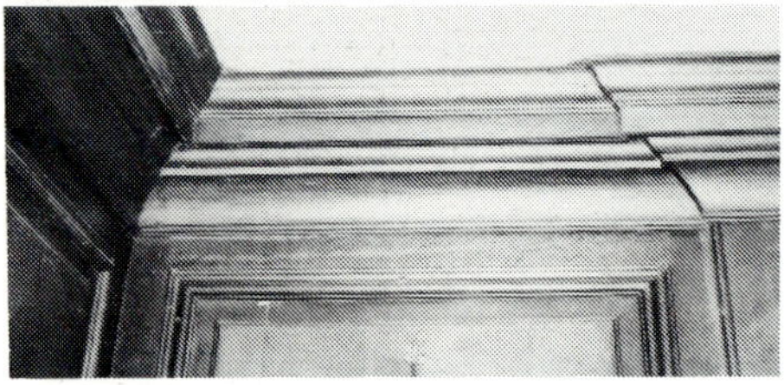

59. *Timber cornice of the last quarter of the 17C. consisting of a cyma, corona, ovolo and cavetto from the top down. Tuscan derivation (see page 19)*

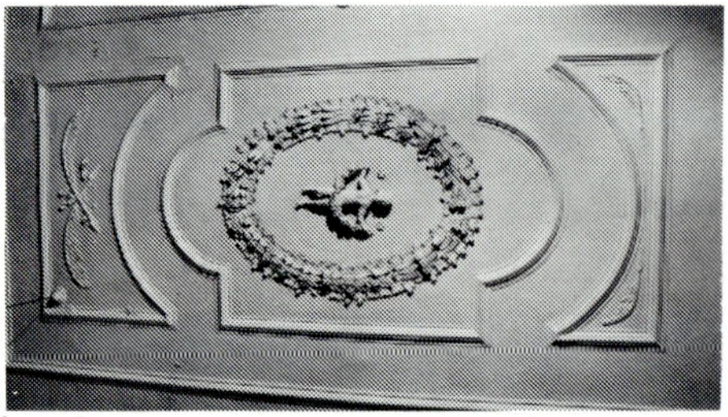

60. *A fine ceiling, probably of the third quarter of the 17C. This kind of ribbed panel layout continues into the Queen Anne period. Note the characteristic cherub in the oval which is modelled in deep relief.*

61.

61. *Detail from ceiling in* **60***. This naïve, deeply sculptured figure probably represents the goddess Flora. The tightly packed oval garland of leaves and flowers is typical of the second half of the 17C.*

62. *Last quarter 17C. Another cornice apparently of Tuscan origin.*

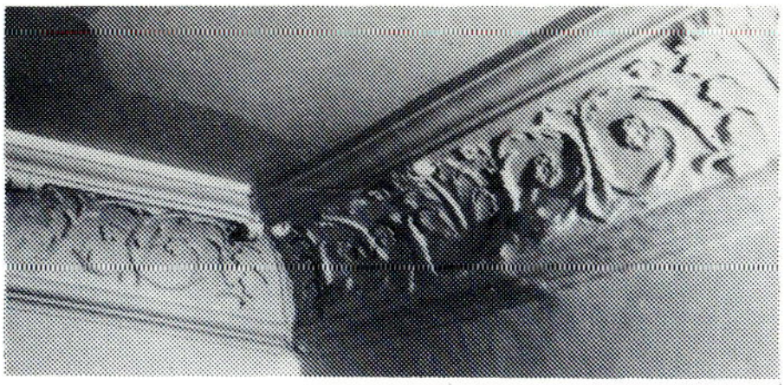

63. *This late 17C. coved 'cornice' with its bold acanthus leaves and floral trail, still has much in common with earlier frieze details. It is fairly typical of its period*

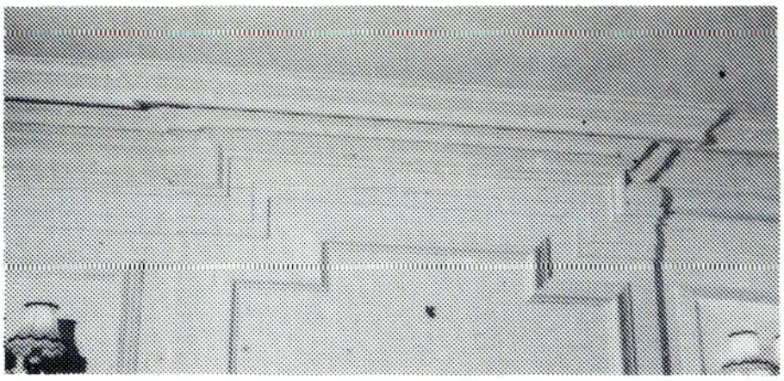

64. *Late 17C. entablature with manneristic touches, like the architrave mouldings which turn upwards to break into the pulvinated frieze.*

65.

65. *Typical of its period, this late 17C. cornice breaks forward to form a chimneypiece feature with panelled pilasters. (see* **70** *below and fireplace pages).*

66. *Late 17C. or early 18C. timber cornice in a pine panelled room.*

66.

67. *Typical Queen Anne ceiling with fairly delicate ribs, arranged in a geometric design of interconnected rectangles and circles.*

68. *Another ceiling from the first quarter of the 18C. The outer rib pattern adopts an almost Gothic outline. Note also the cable moulding of the main rectangle.*

69. *Early 18C. cornice, consisting mainly of a determined-looking cyma recta. This is in the spirit of the bold timber coves often seen under the eaves of buildings at this period.*

70. *Cornice mouldings of c.1710. at the chimneypiece projection. They are still in the late 17C. manner. The ceiling ribs are hardly different from the bolection mouldings of the wall panels.*

71. *Elaborate and forceful plasterwork in a large town house of the 1730's. Although this is a typically Palladian building, the spirit of the ceiling could be described as Baroque, with its vigorously scrolled cartouches and massive ribs of tightly packed fruit and flowers. There is nothing coolly classical about it.*

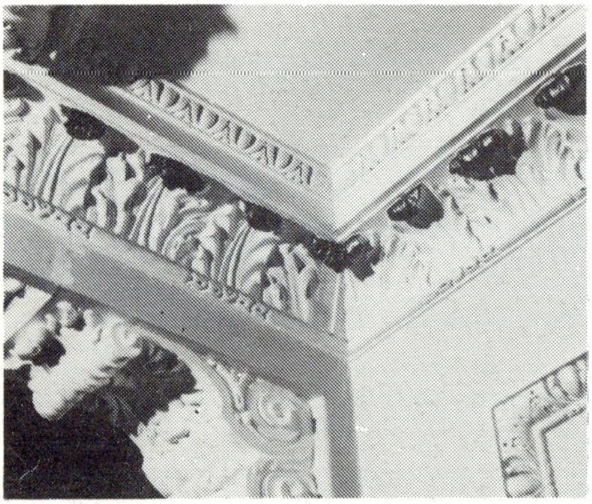

72. *Cornice detail from the same house as* **71** *above (date:-1730's). Note the egg and dart enrichment of the top ovolo. The deep cove with its vigorous acanthus leaves is very reminiscent of the 17C. cornice in* **63**. *The moulding at the bottom could be described as "bead and bell-flower".*

73. *Another cornice of the 1730's. This one is Ionic, and reads downwards as:— cyma recta, enriched cyma reversa, corona (and plain band), enriched ovolo, dentils and enriched cyma reversa. But for that extra band it is very correct.*

CEILINGS AND CORNICES

77. *Detail of key fret from ceiling* **78** *(right). c.1725-50.*

78. *Ceiling detail of second quarter 18C. including panel with peacock and garlands. Note the straight rib adjoining the curved one is clasped by a scroll.*

78.

74. *1730's ceiling with arabesques of rococo flavour. The large surrounding ribs are decorated with a swastika version of the key fret, enclosing rosettes.*

79. *(Right). The kind of rococo coved cornice mouldings typical of the 1750's and 60's. Centre of this ceiling* **80** *(below).*

79.

75. *A fine ceiling probably of the second quarter of the 18C. The central arabesque of flat ribbons, reminiscent of Jacobean strapwork, is quite often seen in this period, as are masks and scrolls clasping the rib moulding of the central oval. It is very like a Batty Langley design of 1729.*

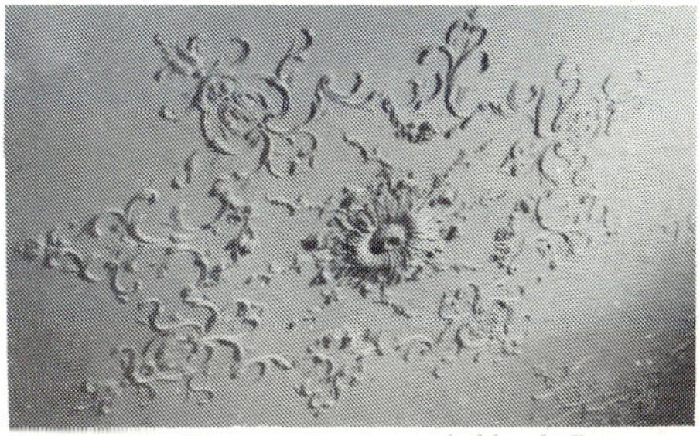

80. *Typical ceiling centre, surrounded by shallow arabesques of highly stylised ornament, frequently used in the third quarter of the 18C. The spirit is rococo. Cornice* **79** *above is in the same room.*

76. *Corner detail of ceiling* **75** *above, of about 1725-50. The key fret enclosing rosettes is typical of the period, but was also used both earlier and later.*

81. *Simple coved cornice of the 1770's, which would not be too difficult to get made. It consists of a cyma recta, big cavetto and an astragal. Overall depth 5 inches and maximum horizontal projection 4 inches.*

CEILINGS AND CORNICES

82. *Typical Corinthian cornice of the 1770's, complete but for a row of dentils. Reads downwards as:— cyma recta, cyma reversa, corona, and bed mould of modillions and rosettes, egg and dart enriched ovolo and a cavetto.*

83. *This flat looking "cornice" of the 1770's is really a key pattern frieze, rounded off at the bottom with a cable mould and capped by an egg and dart ovolo.*

84. *Although loosely described as a "cornice", this example of the 1770's really constitutes a vastly simplified entablature with Adamesque swags in the frieze. It is typical.*

85. *A late 18C. cornice which would be relatively easy to copy. It has a cyma recta at the top, then a small cyma reversa, a corona, cavetto and astragal.*

86. *This cornice is typical of developments at the end of the 18C. and beginning of the 19C. A flat band of running decoration appears on the ceiling.*

87. *Early 19C. stylised bands of corn and leaves, with fleurons at the corners, adorn the ceiling. The cornice is now just a row of curled acanthus leaves.*

88. *Crisp early 19C. ceiling band consisting of a wheat and leaf trail with rosettes at the corners. The "cornice" is a row of sloping acanthus, separated by a torus moulded fillet from egg and dart ovolo and a bead-and-reel astragal.*

89.

89. *This Regency ceiling of c.1814 has banded decoration of rosettes in circles linked by bead mouldings. A conventional cornice, reading rather like* **69** *surmounts the sunk wall panelling.*

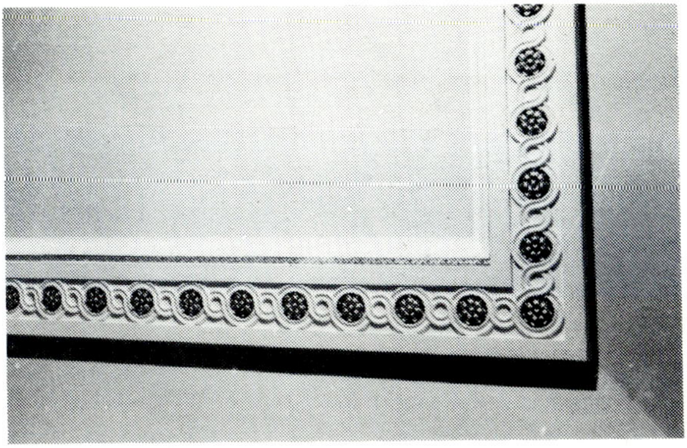

90.

90. *Probably dating from the second quarter of 19C., this guilloche ceiling band, flanked by plain fillets, contains gilded rosettes. The ceiling is coved in the "saloon" style. The band decorates the change in plane between coved and flat surfaces. Stylistically it could just as well date from the late 18C.*

91.

91. *A good early 19C. "cornice" consisting of a vine leaf and grapes trail ceiling band, bounded on one side by a sloping row of acanthus, and supported on the other by free standing Greek acanthus and other stylised leaves.*

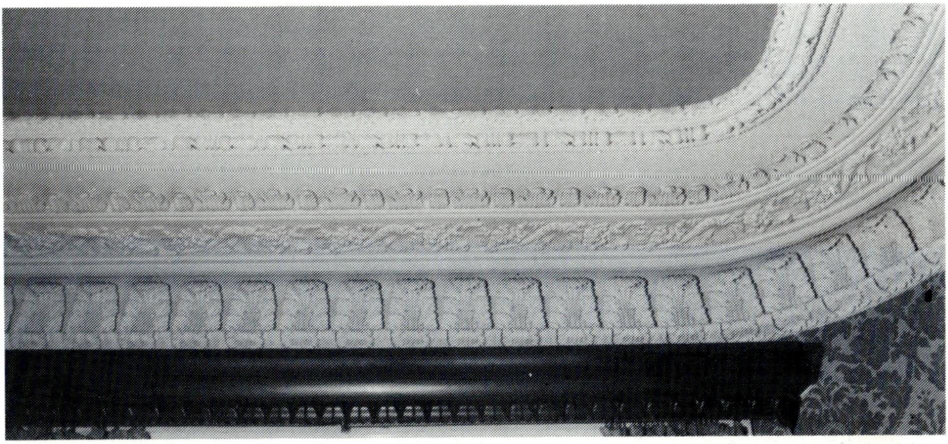

92. *A monumental cornice of the 1840's. Huge curled acanthus leaves support a vine trail which differs little from that in* **91** *above. Indeed it may have been cast in the same moulds. Further acanthus leaves rise to a plain cove, which is bordered by bead and reel mouldings.*

CEILINGS AND CORNICES

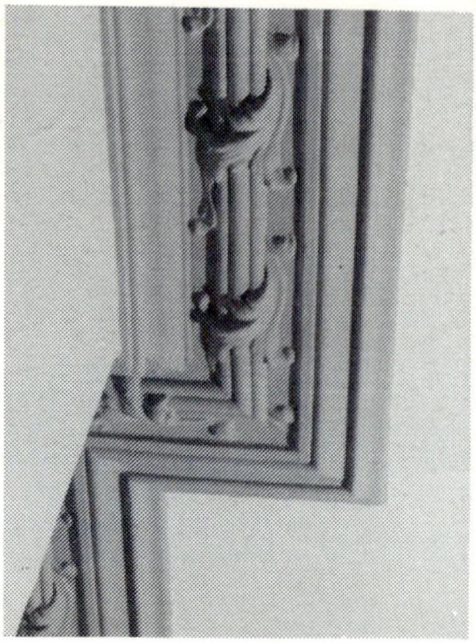

94. *Cornice and ceiling mouldings of the 1860's, consisting of an ogee, bordering a cluster of beads wound with artifical foliage.*

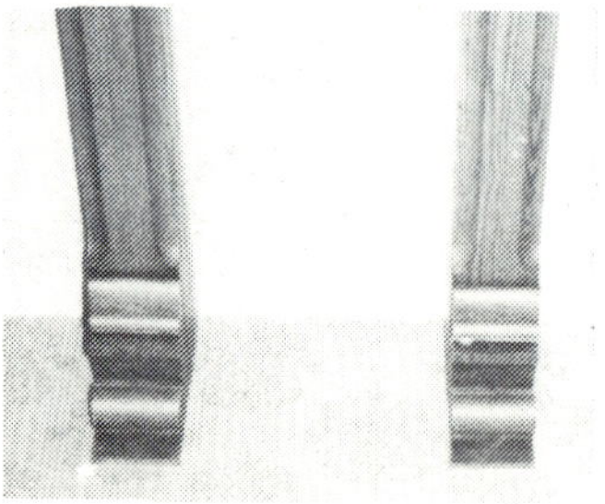

93. *Early Victorian plasterwork of the1840's. Elaborate ornament appears in surprising places, like the convex moulding of the cornice, enriched with a ribbon bound trail of flowers. The flowers can apparently be unscrewed. The ceiling band has now separated from the cornice, and sports a corner device of anthemion and scrolled tendrils.*

95. *These varnished beams of the second half of the 19C. rest on timber corbels, and are decorated with deep hollow chamfers. They are in a style which derives from French châteaux.*

96. *Edwardian ceiling mouldings of c.1900. The frieze has a motif of swags in the Georgian revival manner favoured at this time.*

97. *Where softwood joists in old cottages are to be left exposed, you cannot do better than paint them with white emulsion. They lighten a low room, but do not draw attention to themselves. Unlike gloss paint, emulsion does not "yellow".*

98. *The kind of ceiling centre of swirling stylised foliage which was used again and again in the second half of the 18C.*

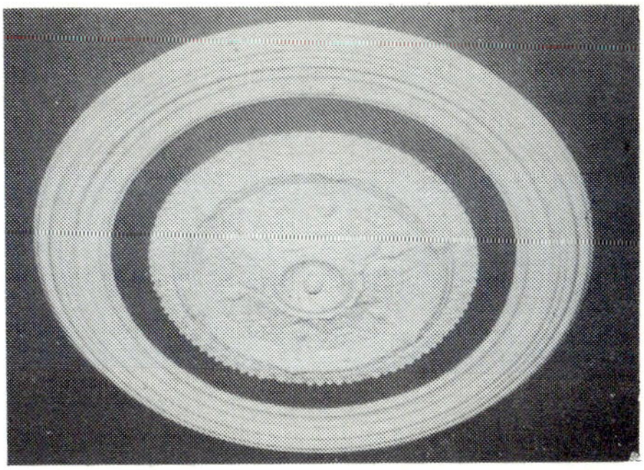

99. *Early to mid-19C. centre, surrounded by a deeply modelled circular rib moulding of a section seen on tondo and oval picture frames.*

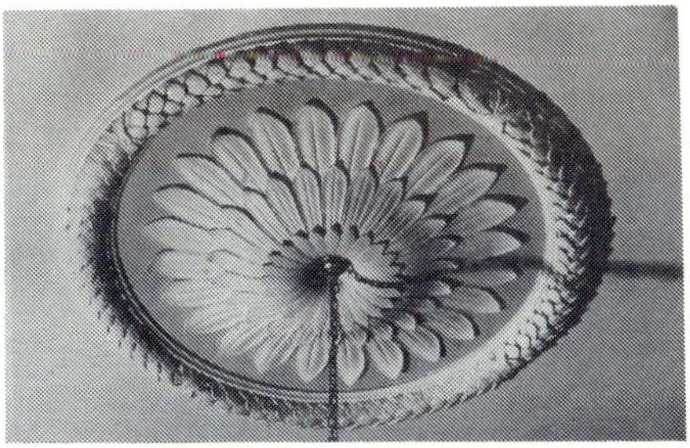

100. *Regency centre c.1810 with tight radiating circles of laurel leaves, surrounded by a stiff looking bay leaf garland. It has a French Empire look about it.*

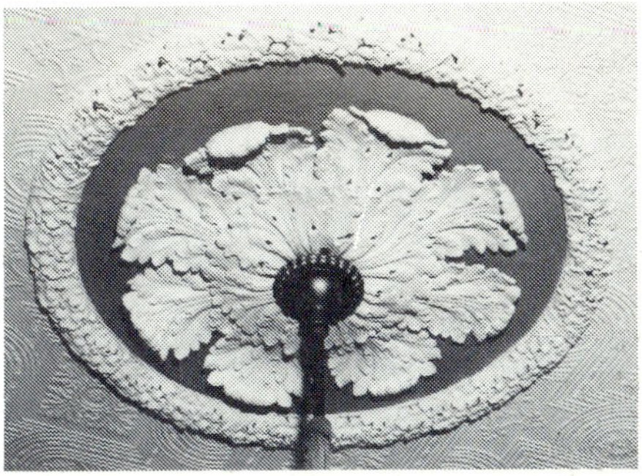

101. *Centre of c.1810 with very blunt, and curled over acanthus leaves and a circular garland.*

102. *Ceiling centre of the 1840's. Acanthus and laurel centre. Palmette motif in the band. Outer ring of acanthus leaves.*

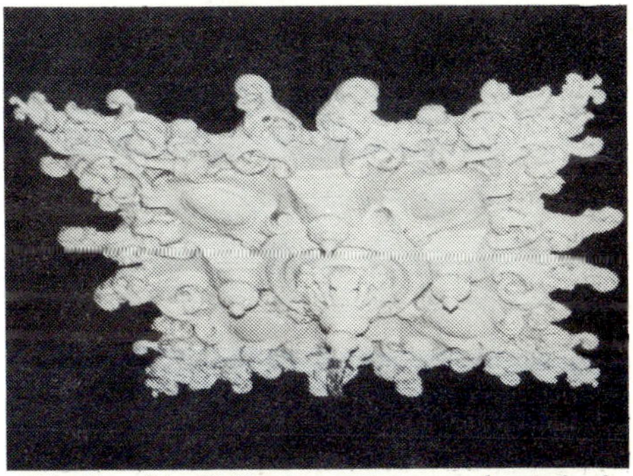

103. *Also of the 1840's, this suggests several periods of decoration. The cable moulding around the central pendant is 18C. The pendants themselves could be Jacobean, while the lozenge centred cartouches are 17C. Baroque devices. The violent surrounding foliage is reminiscent of Gothic carving.*

104. *Acanthus and palmette centre of the 1860's.*

FLOORS

105.

105. *Flagstones set diagonally in the Great Hall of the National Trust's Trerice — late 16C.*

106. *Floor of seashore pebbles, dated 1638, in the cross-passage of a house with Elizabethan, medieval and Norman phases of construction.*

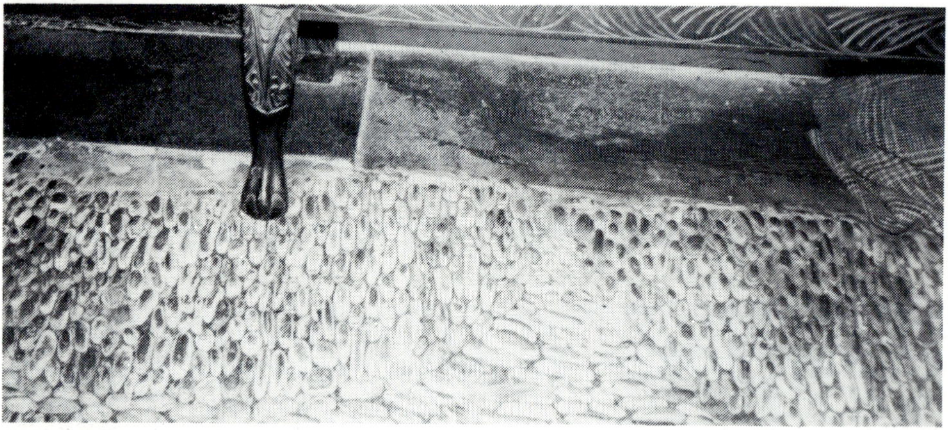

106.

107.

107. *A fine mid-17C. brick floor laid in stretcher bond. The depression filled with granite is where a stream flowed through the house. It is said that people used it to clean off their shoes before entering the main living quarters.*

108. *Oak parquet quarter landing of a late 17C. staircase. Landings were often treated in this way.*

108.

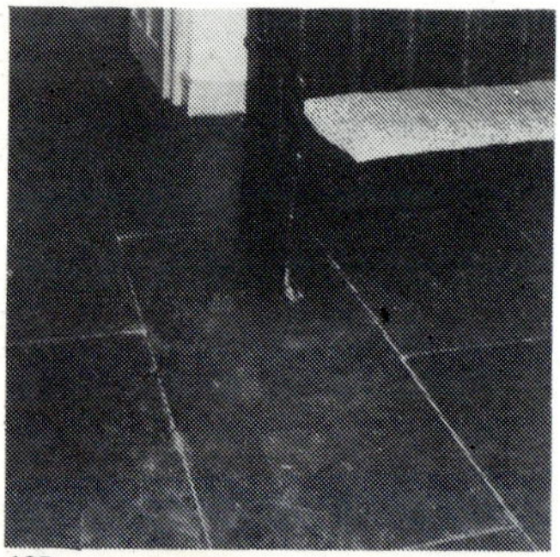

109.

109. *Huge slate flagstones — a splendid floor finish for halls, kitchens, larders and laundries.*

110. *Rough granite flagstones in a late 17C. or early 18C. cottage. Here a millstone has been used to fill space — beneath the settle.*

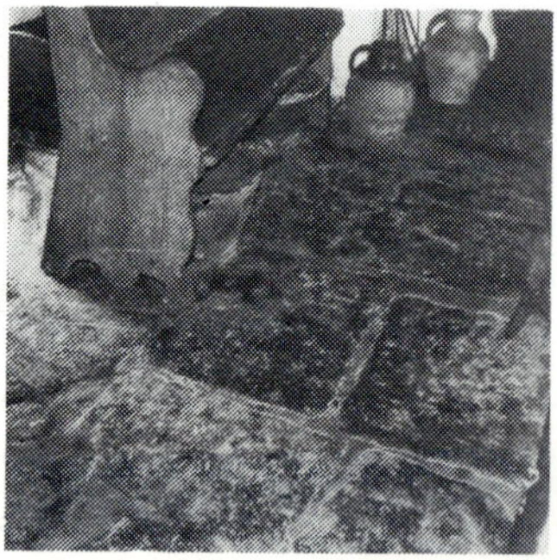

110.

111. *Today, strip flooring, like this, is more often laid in hardwood on a solid mortar screed, but it is sometimes used upstairs to cover existing boards, or may be so arranged that ends butt together over joists for nailing.*

112. *Granite flagstones in a passage of a Queen Anne house.*

112.

113.

113. *These softwood boards in a late 18C. vicarage have been given the dry-scrubbed look. The original method was to scatter damp sand to pick up the dust and fluff. This was then brushed up again. Next, sweet smelling herbs and petals were broadcast over the floor and brushed in hard. Finally, the remains of the herbs, etc., were swept off the floor.*

114.

114. *Flagstones in the staircase hall of an early 19C. rebuild of a 17C. house.*

115. *Modern red clay quarry tiles. These are a good option for owners of old houses.*

115.

117. *Modern clay tiles in a cottage kitchen. A useful finish which is both practical and in keeping.*

118. *Hardwood mosaic panels, wax polished, can prove a relatively cheap and inoffensive floor finish. They are very similar to parquet, and look less busy in reality than they do in photographs. They are certainly all right in undistinguished houses.*

118

116. *A typical late Victorian-Edwardian tiled floor in a sharply geometric pattern. Thousands of houses have them, but since they are characteristic of their period, they are often worth keeping.*

119. *Polished concrete flagstones in the hall of an early 19C. cottage. These can be surprisingly effective, provided the pointing is toned in and the right colours are chosen. If of the wrong colour or texture, or used in the wrong building, they could be a disaster.*

119.

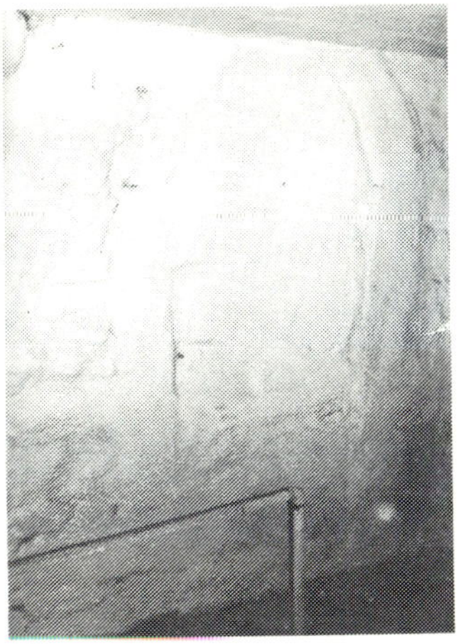

120.

120. *The ghost of a blocked-up Medieval doorway, with pointed arch, can be seen in the cross passage of this early 15C. hall-house. The kind of thing to look for and reinstate.*

121.

121. *Oak framed doorway revealed during work on a later 16C. stone building with Tudor gatehouse. The jambs have been roughly shaped to form an arch and are morticed, tenoned and pegged into the head.*

12 .

122. *Late 15C. pattern of door. Three broad planks are spiked to a framework of stiles, rails and muntins, using big, square-headed nails. The framing is simply scratch moulded, but the outer corners have probably been mitred when replacement top and bottom rails were inserted. Pale horizontal marks on the frame are from laths nailed across when it was once plastered over. Strap hinges are typically sandwiched between plank and frame.*

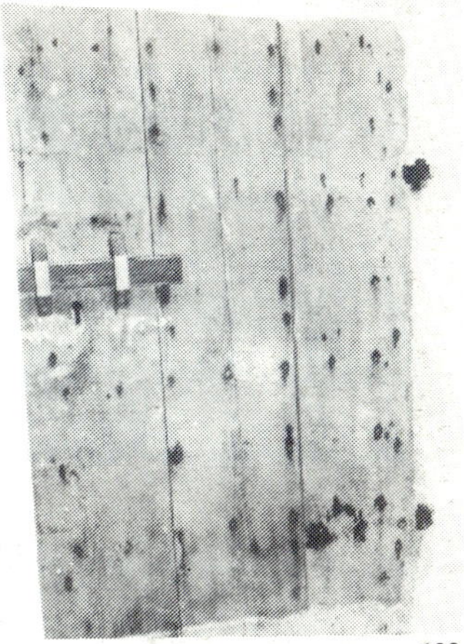

123.

123. *Other side of late 15C. door in* **122** *(left). The rust marks are where the nails are clenched over. Note the hinges are hung on gudgeon pins sunk into the stone jambs. The suitable wooden bolt is modern.*

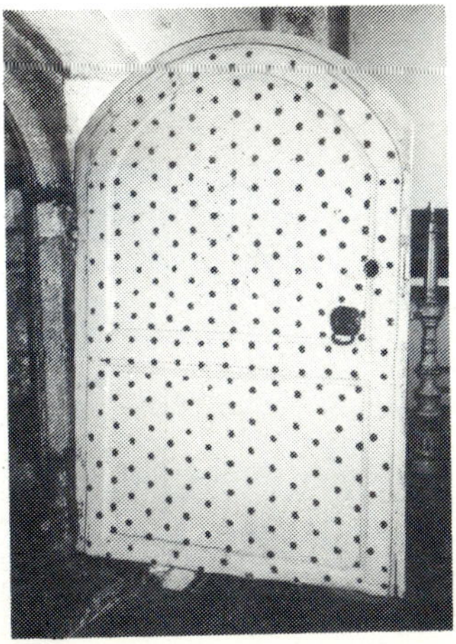

124.

124. *Door of triple construction in a 15C. church. A frame with ogee mouldings forms two big panels. This is applied to wide vertical boards, which are, in turn, laid over horizontal ones. All are fixed together by large wrought-iron nails, with very roughly made heads. The whole method of construction is early; but the details suggest that it is not as ancient as it first appears.*

125.

125. *Inside of door* **124** *(left). These hinges are probably not original but are of convincing design. The bottom one is of the "harr" type, terminating in a stout pin socketed into the granite threshold.*

DOORS

126.

126. *This fine granite arch with its heavy roll moulding is of the early 16C.*

127. *Plain granite arch with wide chamfer having "pyramid" stops. It leads to a typical straight flight of stone steps (carpeted) running parallel to the rear wall of the building. Late 16C.*

128. *Late 16C. front door from a cross passage into a two-storied porch. It is of double construction — vertical boards on the outside and horizontal ones inside.*

127.

128.

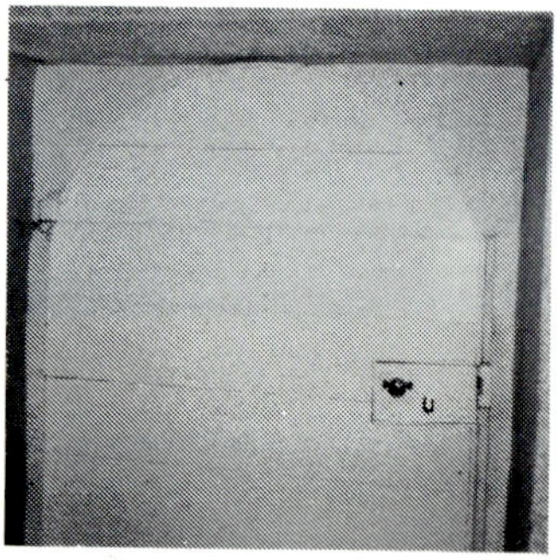

129. *The inside of late 16C. door* **128** *(left). Wide horizontal boards form the inner skin. Rim lock is probably 18C. or early 19C.*

130. *Detail of late 16C. door* **128** *(left). Note the typical bead mouldings. The stud-headed nails and the crude strap hinge. The knocker is of a pattern used in the 18th and 19C. and much reproduced in the 20C.*

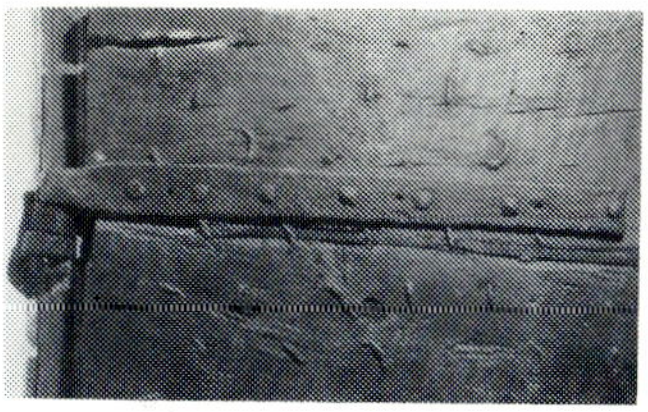

131. *Detail of door in* **134** *(below), clearly shows marks of the adze used to shape the boards, and how the ends of the nails are clenched over. The strap hinge has no distinguishable features, but is convincing.*

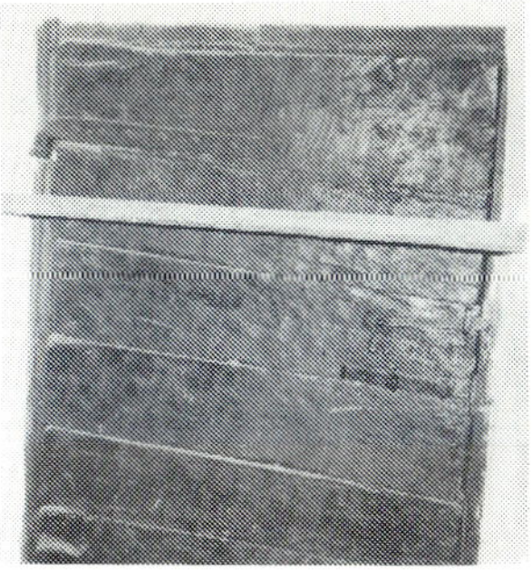

132. *Early form of security, a timber pole slid into sockets in the jamb stones. This feature could be 16C. or earlier.*

133. *Detail of door furniture of* **134** *(below left). The shaped loop handle and latch are typical of a type seen at the end of 16C. and beginning of 17C. Likewise, the bolt with its simple incised cross decoration.*

134.

134. *This oak door could be either 16C. or 17C. The strap hinges with their shaped ends and bevelled edges are hung on pins attached to a frame, unlike those in* **128**. *The long bolt, whatever its age, is held by three wrought-iron butterfly staples of the kind used in the 16C. and 17C.*

135.

135. *Doorway of late 16C. type with four-centre arch in the National Trust's Trerice. It is made of limestone, and has a wide chamfer with pyramid stops.*

136.

136. *Reverse of 16C. door in* **137** *(right). Some of the ledges have been renewed. The latch with its sneck is of the thumb lift type. The wooden stock lock is possibly 19C. and appears to replace a timber bolt.*

137.

137. *Plank door (much repaired) in the roof space partition of a 16C. manor house. The blunt and spear-ended strap hinges are hung on iron pins spiked into the frame. The handle is a thumb latch type seen from the 17C. onwards.*

DOORS

138.

138. *Granite arched doorway c.1612 onto a pebble floored cross passage. The door is of a convincing pattern with moulded vertical ribs covering the joints between boards.*

139.

139. *Ledged door in a Jacobean manor house. Wooden stock lock is probably 19C. Timber latch is of uncertain date, but suitable design.*

140.

140. *The construction of this door suggests the mid-17C. It has a panel frame of stiles, muntins and rails with mitred joints and ovolo mouldings. Faceted, stud-headed nails are driven through to the vertical boards behind. These, in turn, are held together by horizontal ledges. The fleur-de-lis ended strap hinges were still used in the 17C. although of much earlier origin. The loop handle on an iron backplate is again, of correct design. The door frame is ovolo moulded with tongue stops. As an authentic pattern, the door makes sense: but it must be remembered that doors were often faithfully copied or repaired in the 19C; and re-hung in the original or earlier frames.*

141.

141. *Inside door* **140** *(left). Three wide planks are held together with chamfered ledges. A huge timber stock lock has been re-fitted (?) on its side.*

142.

142. *This fine old door has been scratched and worn away by centuries of impatient dogs. It is probably mid 17C. but the strap hinges could be earlier. The wood has had a coat of some kind of bitumen paint.*

143. *Detail of strap hinges from* **142** *(left). Note the scratched decoration at and near the tip. It is fixed with faceted, stud-headed nails. It could be late 16C. or early 17C.*

144.

144. *Magnificent early 17C. doorway of primitive, classical design in the Jacobean idiom. The mannerist brackets of the boldly reeded frieze and the arcaded panels between downward tapering pilasters, are all redolent of the transitional style of c.1600 — 1640. The paired columns with diamond-pointed rustication and Ionic caps are also typical.*

145. *Late 17C. door with typical baroque scrolled pediment and Tête d'Ange device with crossed wings. The two panel arrangement with strong bolection mouldings and H-L hinges are also characteristic.*

145.

146.

146. *Another late 17C. doorway. Note the segmental pediment, pulvinated frieze and broad, flat architrave divided into two fascias.*

147. *The alternative late 17C. and early 18C. door architrave is this kind with a bold bolection moulding. Both door and brass rim lock are right for the period. Note also the typical cornice mouldings above; and the wall panel mouldings.*

147.

DOORS

148.

148. *Last quarter 17C. Another popular layout for panels at this time was to sandwich an horizontal between two larger vertical ones. Note the pulvinated frieze. The hinges are of the 'H-L' type with one side of the 'H' nailed inside the doorcase like a butt hinge.*

149. *Queen Anne door (c.1702-14) of a pattern frequently seen in French buildings. The curved tops of the doors, the paired panes of glass and the proportions are all continental. Note the sturdy glazing bars, the faceted spandrel motifs and bolection moulded architrave.*

149.

150.

150. *Plain early 18C. door with bolection moulded architrave rising from solid plinth blocks at skirting level (c.1702-14).*

151.

151. *Doorcase in a house of the 1730's. The shouldered architrave breaks upwards in the middle and is capped by an ogee moulded cornice.*

152. *This hall archway probably dates from the second quarter of the 18C. The arch moulding has a dropped key block echoed by a cornice which breaks outwards to make a feature. The arch springs from a cyma moulded architrave which is returned around the linings of the opening, giving the impression of a pilaster.*

152.

153. *This is an under-stairs cupboard door in a town house of the 1770's. Note the 'H-L' nailed hinge still in use. Panel mouldings are small ovolos. The latch is typical of a type used at this date and in the early 19C. See 167b.*

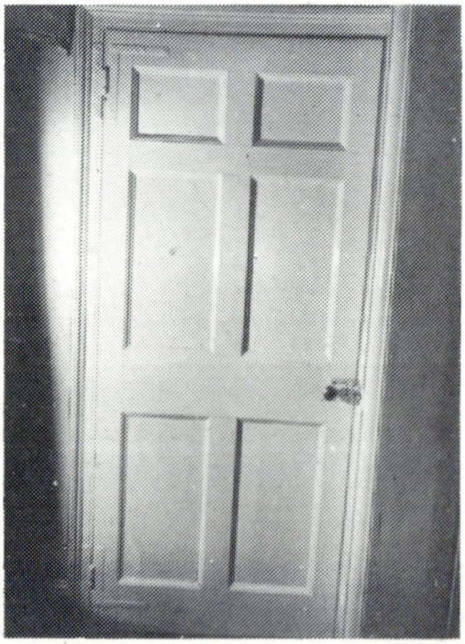

153.

154.

154. *Hall archway of the late 18C. or early 19C. A plain semi-circular arch, with panelled soffit, springs from simple pilasters with straightforward cap mouldings.*

155.

155. *Early 19C. jib door in the wainscotting of a staircase hall. Note the moulded skirting, plain dado, and the rather flat looking chair rail, with a fascia between two mouldings.*

156.

156. *Characteristic early 19C. door and architrave. The reeded architrave, stopped at the corners with squares containing roundels, is seen everywhere in houses from 1800 to about 1840. The door is of fine mahogany, with a key-cornered panel above the lock rail.*

157.

157. *This style of ogee, crocketed overdoor (of 14C. decorated derivation) could belong to any stage of Gothic revival architecture, from Horace Walpole's Strawberry Hill of the 1750's to the early 19C.*

158.

158. *Regency door (c.1813) with low lock rail and six panels of almost equal size, hung on three butt-hinges. The middle fascia of the architrave is typically reeded.*

159.

159. *Fine quality joinery of the 1840's. The door and door case are curved. Note the square end blocks in the frieze containing fleurons — a popular device at this time, replacing Regency roundels. The pilaster to the right is Corinthian.*

160.

160. *Eclectic doorcase of 1840's. The cornice and acanthus filled frieze are supported by brackets of Renaissance flute and ball decoration, terminated by bold acanthus leaves. The architrave has three fascias and the 'pilasters' are fluted and reeded. The four panels of the door have heavy ogee mouldings. Door plate see* **167D**.

161.

161. *Plain four-panel door of c.1860. The architrave has a simple convex moulding and two fascias. The panel mouldings are finished with a bead.*

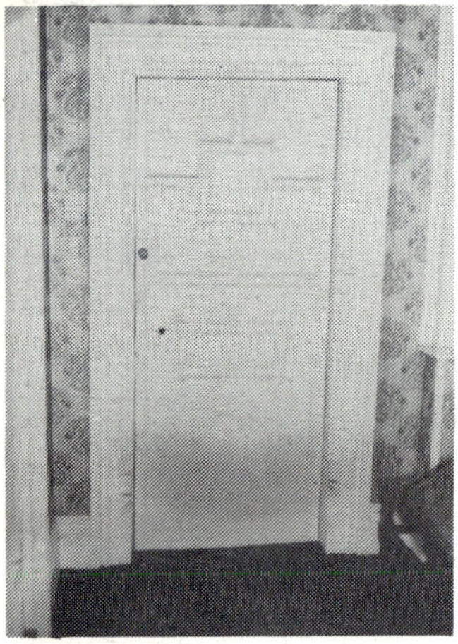

162.

162. *Second half of 19C. Victorian Jacobean. The typical square design of c.1585-1630 fades out further down the door. The architrave has a version of late 17C. bolection mouldings, stopped in an earlier manner.*

163.

163. *Victorian (second half 19C.) Tudoresque oak linenfold door.*

164.

164. *Tudor arch of Victorian vintage.*

165.

165. *A suitable new door for 18C. and 19C. cottages. It is ledged-and-braced and hung from plain 1¼" thick linings, with ironmongers japanned 'T' hinges. Latch, see* **167g**. *The depth and thickness of the ledges should be increased for 17C. and earlier buildings and braces omitted.* **See 135, 139, 142**. *It could be argued that the ledges and braces of this example are a little mean.*

HINGES

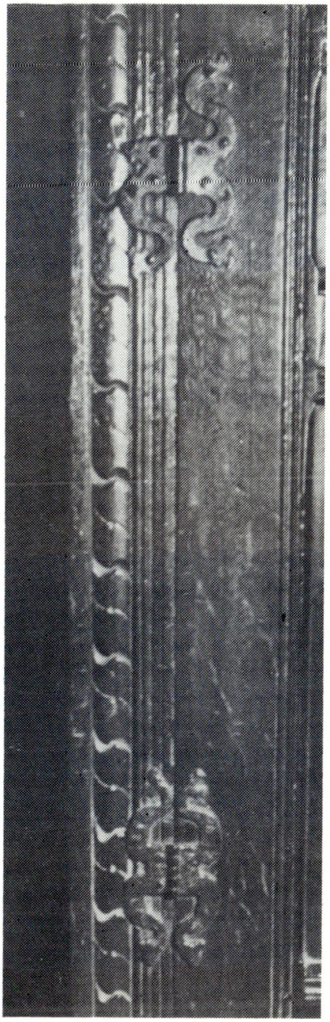

a. *The cocks-head hinge was often used in the late 16th and early 17th centuries.*

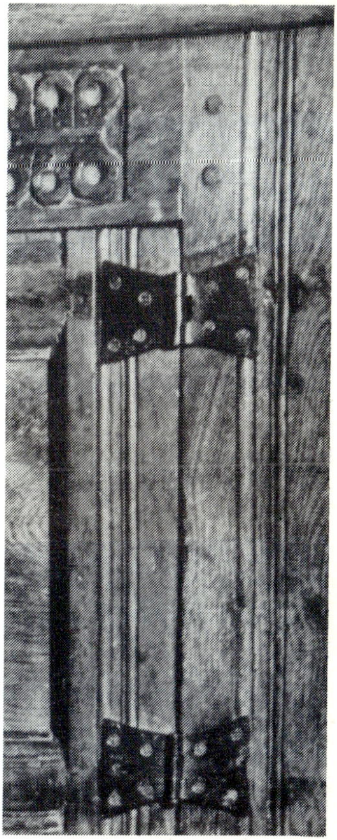

b.

b. *Butterfly hinges were popular, for smaller doors like those of cupboards during the late 16th and all of the 17th. century. Unlike these, which could be replacements, they were fixed with round headed nails.*

c.

c. *The commonest internal door hinge in the 17th and early 18th centuries was the 'H' type fixed with hand-wrought nails with fairly large heads. The ends of the hinge were often shaped and the edges chamfered.*

d. *Another hinge often employed in the late 17th and much of the 18th centuries, was the 'H-L' type. Sometimes, one arm of the hinge was turned to fix inside instead of on the face of the frame.*

a. Timber stock-lock with iron mounts, staple and key escutcheon. Probably Victorian.

b. Spring hatchet latches were often used in the 18C. This is a late version on a square back plate, and could even by early 19C. One arm of the spring is missing.

c. Brass rim lock of typical 18C pattern with a drop handle. Details apart, this kind of lock was used in the 17C and on into 19C as well. Late ones were often black japanned, with brass trimmings.

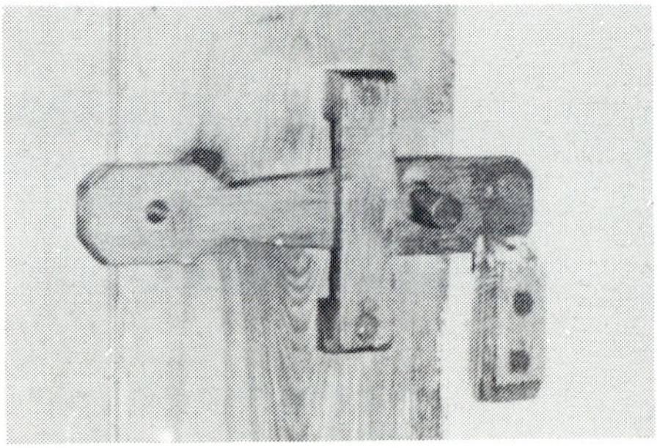

d. A modern timber latch suitable for a cottage cupboard door.

e.

e. Brass door plate with swags and musical trophy. Other, copper art nouveav ones, in the same house came from Liberty's and no doubt date from about 1900.

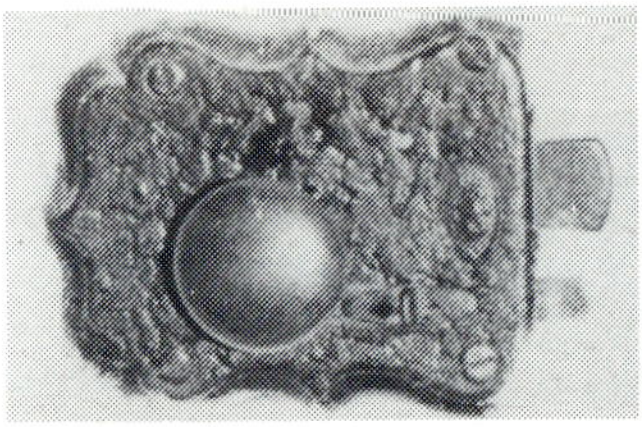

f. This little japanned latch with brass knob is probably later 19C.

g. The modern ironmongers' black japanned rim latch with a brass handle must be about the most useful and suitable fitting for late 18C and 19C cottage doors' apart from the thumb-latch.

168.

168. *Early 16C. granite newel stair of fine quality. Each beautifully dressed step keys in with the next like the vertebrae of a skeleton.*

169.

169. *Unlike* **168**, *this spiral stair is formed of wedge shaped granite winders supported by a solid core of masonry in a rectangular staircase wing. It is probably 16C.*

170.

170. *Granite arch leading to* **169**. *Probably 16C. it has broad, unstopped chamfers.*

171.

171. *Mid 17C. oak open well staircase — an early example of its kind, with turned balusters resting on the string and a heavy handrail, which is deeper than it is wide. The ball finials typically have an incised line of turning and are not true spheres. A few late 16C. staircases with balustrades may be found which share some of these characteristics.*

172.

172. *Mast newel stair with winders housed into a stout post, rising up through the building. This type is often seen in the 16C. and the first part of the 17C.*

173.

173. *A mid to late 17C. type of oak staircase with ovolo moulded and stopped newels, and flat bun finials. The vase turned balusters are fairly stocky and rest on the closed string.*

174.

174. *Top landing balustrade of* **173**, *dating from the second half of the 17C.*

175. *This staircase presents some conflicting points of style. Balanced opposing flights, together with classically detailed panelled posts and pulvinated strings, all suggest the second half of the 17C. The shaped arch is a feature more often seen in the late 16C and early 17C, but can be much later. Dog gates with fretted balusters are often Jacobean. These, however, echo the outline of the turned ones on the stairs.*

176.

176. *Balustrade detail from* **175**. *Note the strong similarity in the turning of these and both the Elizabethan balusters in* **171** *and the early 18C. ones in* **185**.

177. *Late 17C open-well stairs with Baroque influenced loose-twist balusters on vase turnings. The pulvinated string and panelled newel with moulded cap are also typical.*

177.

179. *Pine string of staircase* **178** *with hardwood turned balusters rested on it.*

178. *Late 17C tight open-well staircase with plain newels, moulded handrail and strings in pine. The balusters, finials and pendants are in hardwood.*

180.

180. *Foot of late 17C. oak staircase. Note the newly introduced cut-string with balusters standing on the treads, the carved brackets, and thai the handrail finishes on top of the panelled newel.*

181.

181. *The handrail of staircase* **180** *is made up of a pronounced central roll flanked by further convex mouldings.*

182.

182. *This is the same staircase shown in* **180** *and* **181**. *The handrail is now carried over the newel at changes of direction; and given a knee-and-ramp to adjust to the change of level.*

183.

183. *This staircase, in a Queen Anne house (c. 1702-14), while quite possible contemporary, is clearly of the late 17C. pattern. Compare with* **177**.

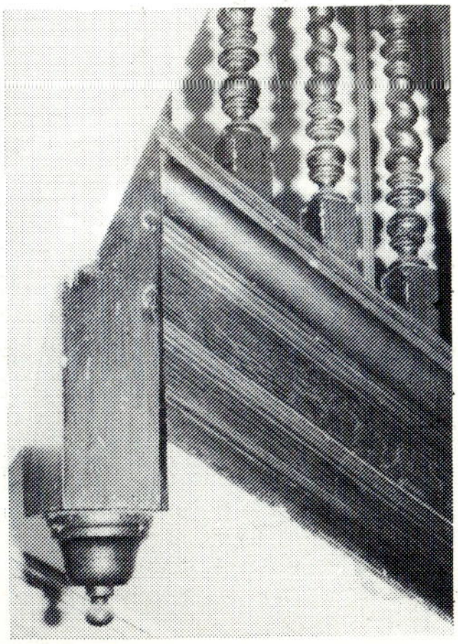

184.

184. *Turned newel pendant to staircase* **183** . *The string is peg-jointed into the newel and is decorated with a cavetto, ogee and bead mouldings.*

185.

185. *This sturdy little back staircase in a Queen Anne house (c.1702-14) has a plain timber baulk for a handrail and balusters turned in rather the same manner as those in* **176** *and* **171**.

STAIRS

186. *Nearby doors and panelling suggest the late 17C. or early 18C. for this vernacular balustrade in a building which dates back to the late 16C. and possibly earlier still.*

187. *Mahogany staircase of quality in a Palladian house of the 1730's. The closed string, panelled newel, broad flat rail and symmetrically turned balusters are a throwback to Inigo Jones (early 17C.) The baluster design was widely used long before that by Italian Renaissance artists and architects.*

187.

188.

188. *Plain staircase of 1730's with moulded handrail and newel cap. The slim balusters rest on the closed string and have adopted a column-on-vase outline.*

189. *A type of staircase often seen in the second quarter of the 18C. This has an open string and brackets, a curtail step on which stands a fluted "Doric" newel, wreathed handrail and column-on-vase balusters.*

189.

190.

190. *This staircase is possible c. 1760's but conforms in many ways with earlier patterns, having square capped newels and closed strings.*

191. *Open string, bracketed staircase of the 1770's with column-on-vase balusters and newels; and very plain mahogany handrail.*

191.

192.

192. *Typical town house staircase of the 1770's consisting of winding steps with shaped brackets. The mahogany handrail wreaths around to finish on a Doric newel, rising from a curtail step. The balusters are now slim columns on urn or vase bases.*

193. *Mahogany balustraded open string staircase c.1780's. This open string has 'S' brackets with guttae derived from the Doric entablature. The balusters are now of square section and decorated on each face with a single flute.*

193.

194.

194. *The kind of cantilevered geometric staircase with wrought or cast-iron balustrade and bracketed steps favoured in the late 18C. and early 19C. The mahogany handrail is tightly scrolled over an iron newel post rising from a curtail step.*

195. *Shaped landing balustrade in a Regency house c.1814. The cast-iron balustrade is in one of the popular stylised designs of the period.*

195.

196.

196. *With its characteristic plain square balusters, simply turned newel post and moulded mahogany handrail, this staircase is c.1815-1845. Handrails like this however, are also seen in late 18C houses.*

197. *Elegant little staircases like this one may be seen in everything from a modest terraced house to a Regency rectory. They date anywhere from about 1800 to 1840. The plain square balusters and curtail step are typical. One or two balusters in each flight are often made of iron for extra strength.*

197.

STAIRS

198.

198. *This staircase, in a fundamentally much earlier house, is difficult to date, other than to place it in the first half of the 19C. The heavy cast-composition newel looks William IV or early Victorian. The iron balustrade is of a type often used in the late 18th and early 19C.*

199.

199. *Staircase of a small house c1830-60. The balusters are still square, but the turning of the newel looks rather heavier than in the Regency type.*

200.

200. *Dog leg staircase in a small cottage-farmhouse. Date:— second quarter of 19C. The handrail in this case is round and the domed newel caps closely resemble the roundels of the 19C. architrave of similar date. (see* **156** *).*

201.

201. *This staircase of the 1840's continues the Regency tradition, but the balusters are now turned, a bit like late 18C. ones. The dado decoration in the background is Edwardian.*

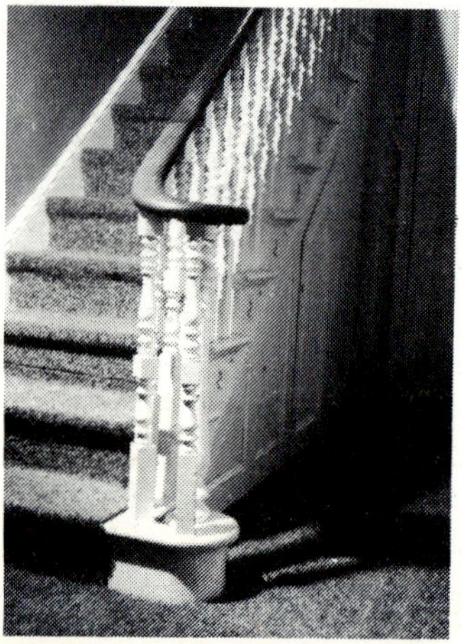

202.

202. *By c.1860 the Regency style has hardly changed, except for the much more fussy turning of the balusters. These are a doubled-up version of a vase shape often seen in the 1720's.*

203.

203. *The very model of a late Victorian or Edwardian balustrade. The spindly balusters contrast with a robust and heavily turned newel, capped by a large block into which the handrail is jointed. The acorn finial is a characteristic embellishment.*

204. *Probably of the second half of the 15C., this fireplace is clearly derived from a much earlier medieval type with a pyramid shaped hood. The back has, at some time, been unbuilt to form a window. The chamfered granite jamb stones, rounded corbels and massive lintel were painted over by a former owner.*

205. *Early 16C granite fireplace with a four-centred arch and spandrels. The strong roll moulding and hollow chamfer give a distinctive rounded effect at the corners, often seen in late medieval examples.*

206. *Like 205 (above right) this early 16C granite fireplace has a heavy roll moulding, but this time it is carried up in the centre to form a decorative peak, containing a ball motif, more often associated with the late 16C and early 17C.*

207. *A typical late 16C fireplace with cambered oak lintel, inglenook seats and a niche to stand an ale mug or salt box. The lintel has previously been hacked as a key for plaster.*

208. *In better quality houses during all the 16C and the early 17C the four-centred Tudor arch predominated. This one is in limestone, has sunk spandrels and the hollow chamfer is typically stopped rather more than one third of the way up the jamb. (2nd half 16C).*

208a. *The earthenware cloam oven was manufactured from the late 17C right through into the 1930's, like this one on display at Truro Pottery (formerly Lake's). They were built into the side of the hearth. A fire was lit inside the oven and was allowed to burn itself out. Then the ashes were raked out and the dough was put in to bake by residual heat. The oven door was sealed around with clay during baking.*

209

209. *(left) Elizabethan chimneypieces like this one of 1573 in the National Trust's Trerice, became partly classical, having cornices, friezes and architraves. The male figures (Atlantes) are classically derived, and strapwork in the central panel is a device from the European pattern books.*

210. *(above) Also from Trerice, this fireplace of 1572 again shows Renaissance details at a transitional stage of development. The "terms" suporting the upper entablature are characteristic of the period.*

211

211. *(left) This exuberantly carved oak fireplace is typical of work in the late 16th and early 17th centuries. The bracketed entablature and manneristic "terms" are characteristic of Renaissance architecture freely adapted by Flemish and German treatise writers like Vredeman de Vries and Wendel Dietterlin. In this example, the "terms" flanking the fireplace opening, although of similar date, have been cleverly added to replace missing ones. The metal smoke-shutter is a temporary expedient; and the pierced fender raised on cast paw feet is of a type seen in the early 19C.*

212. *16C granite fireplace with bold chamfered jambs and lintel. The height of the hearth indicates that the floor level has been lowered at a later stage of the building's history.*

213. *The length of the great oak lintel reveals the fact that this wide 16C hearth has been partially blocked up. In fact a fine, deep stone bread oven may still be seen inside the embrasure formed by this wall.*

214. *Chamfered granite fireplace in an upstairs room of a 16C house. When they are as plain as this, they are very hard to date; but usually do originate in the 16C or early 17C. In areas where softer and more easily worked freestone was available, a tudor arch was often adopted, for both structural and decorative reasons.*

215. *Granite fireplace of the late 16C with heavy roll moulding flanked by a cavetto. Could the 'hour-glass' stops to the mouldings relate to the still life 'Vanitas' themes which became popular in the Netherlands in the 17C (see "terms explained")? The smoke shutter and fire basket are modern. The fire dogs are of a 17C pattern.*

216. *Wide granite hearth with chamfered jambs and lintel. Impossible to date on style alone, but this one is probably early 17C.*

217. *Typical granite fireplace of the period starting about 1600 and finishing in the 1640's. It is an obvious development of 206 above; but now has right angle corners and chamfers stopped well above the hearth stone. The ball decorations in the spandrels and central peak are very characteristic. The fire basket is modern.*

FIREPLACES

218. *A fine Jacobean fireplace in carved oak with manneristic "terms" and typical lunettes, arcaded panels, shields and floral trail. The hearth jambs and lintel may have been restored, but the four-centred form of the opening is of a type found at the time this house was rebuilt c. 1612. The granite kerb is not contemporary.*

219. *A surviving fireplace from about the first third of the 17C. in a house rebuilt in the early 19C. The diamond-point decoration with it's ball motifs which stop the jamb mouldings are characteristic. The hood is late 19C. or early 20C. and the grate early 19C. The kerb is modern.*

220. *Cottage down-hearth with internal seat, probably late 17C. or early 18C. The ground floor of this vernacular building has been restored and furnished as a museum, mainly using objects associated with 19C. rural life. (Folk museum, Zennor).*

221. *Inglenook seat and built-in oven, left of fireplace 220.*

222. *This fireplace overmantel, with a bolection moulded panel containing a moral inscription, survives in an old farmhouse. Mid to late 17C.*

223. *Late 17C. kitchen basement fireplace with slightly arched and moulded surround, concealing a brick arch. It has its original chimney crane and bread oven.*

224. *This typical late 17C. chimney crane in hearth 223 (left) is of the single movement kind with a twisted wrought-iron brace. It will only move horizontally in a quarter circle.*

225. *17C. bread oven in hearth 223 with iron door. The inside is usually clay lined. A fire is lit inside the oven, and when it has become really hot, the embers are raked out. Then the bread is put in to bake.*

226. *This big fireplace in freestone, with it's four-centred arch is of a 16C. pattern, but it is in a late 17C. house. The shelf and timber surround are not contemporary. The andirons and chimney crane fit the second half of 17C.*

227. *Late 17C. fireplace with characteristic heavy timber bolection moulding, rising from plain plinth blocks. A late 18C. hob grate has been added, and the surrounding space filled with blue-and-white flower pattern tiles of a type used in Holland in the same period.*

228. *Another late 17C. freestone fireplace with bolection mouldings. This one has a cornice-shelf.*

FIREPLACES

229

229. *Late 17C. chimneypiece with typical pilasters and bolection moulded panel, containing its original oil-on-wood painting. These were often carried out by itinerant Dutch and Flemish artists. Usually their brief was to paint a view of the house itself, together with any tree lined avenue, formal gardens or courtyard in front.*

230. *Here the late 17C. chimneypiece has been composed in the form of a Corinthian order of fluted pilasters rising from floor level. The carved swag is typical of the period and is seen again and again in Renaissance work.*

230

231.

231. *Pine bolection moulded fireplace of the type popular in the late 17C and early 18C. The cast iron register grate is c. 1850-60.*

232. *Chimneypiece in a Queen Anne house. The timber panelled upper portion is typical of the late 17C. and early 18C. period. The huge volutes on either side of the opening may be seen in the work of Inigo Jones (1573 — 1652); but also in the second quarter of the 18C. The delicate classical urn and rosettes on the frieze are more often associated with the late 18C. The hob grate is c.1770-1800.*

232

233

233. *The slightly top-heavy appearance of this fireplace, the shape of the frieze with its vigorous Vitruvian scrolls, and the massive shouldered architrave all point to a date in the second quarter of the 18C. It could almost be a cut-down overdoor. Most of the cornice dentils are missing. The tiled grate is modern.*

234. *A typical Palladian continued chimneypiece of the 1730's. Note the marble consoles with their bold shell and flower pendants, the big volutes supporting the mirror panel and the determined triangular pediment. It is all very architectural.*

234

235

235. *Continued chimneypiece of the 1730's with swan-neck broken pediment. The panel above the marble mantel-shelf is intended to contain a painting or mirror. The tiled grate is c.1880-1900.*

236. *This fireplace is probably of the second quarter of the 18C., but would be just as convincing in the 1760's. The oil painting of a sea battle appears to be original to the panel with its projecting corners and supporting stylised leaf scrolls. The spirit of the decoration is rococo. The grate and brick opening are modern.*

236

237. *A typical fireplace of the 1770's in Carrara marble. Pairs, or double pairs, of columns completing a simplified or adapted classical order — in this case Doric — were popular devices in the mid to late 18C.*

238. *Marble fireplaces with classical scenes carved on a tablet in the middle of the frieze were often used in the last third of the 18C. This one shows Aesop's fable "The Fox and the Stork". Note the consoles and flower pendants continue to be favoured.*

239. *Fireplace of late 18C. design with typical frieze containing Roman foliated scrollwork. Pilaster panels have twined ribbon decoration of Adam flavour. The cast-iron register grate is also in the neo-classical style.*

240. *This fireplace in a house of the 1730's has a Gothic flavour to the frieze which would be more commonly seen later in the 18C. However, Batty Langley was publishing Gothic fireplace designs as early as 1751.*

FIREPLACES

241

241. *Whatever the actual date of this fireplace, it is clearly derived from a Robert Adam type of late 18C design. The flutes and paterae in the frieze are particularly characteristic. This kind of fireplace has been extensively copied up to the present day. Grate: Victorian.*

242. *Probably a 19C pastiche, taking fireplace 219, in the same house, as a theme. The curved roll moulding and finial are Gothic. The "eared" corners and arabesque are 18C. The ball and hour glass motif echoes the decoration of the late 16th and early 17C. It is also referred to as the 'dice box' or 'diabolo' stop.*

242

243

243. *This kind of fireplace is normally early 19C, having a reeded surround and corner blocks containing roundels — all topped by a plain shelf. The grate however, is late 18C.*

244. *Early 19C marble fireplace with moulded architrave and corner blocks containing roundel decoration. The free-standing cast iron grate suggests the gothic influences of c.1860.*

244

245

245. *Marble fireplace of a type which is often encountered in the second quarter of the 19C, but can be slightly earlier. The grate is c.1835-50.*

246. *Mid 19C fireplace fitted around a late 18C hob grate.*

246

247. *Marble fireplace of the 1840's. The mantel-shelf has been dropped in the centre in an eccentric manner, leaving the pilasters with their arched panels, standing on either side like individual pedestals. Firehood: modern.*

248. *Mid — 19C fireplace with very plain consoles supporting a deep shelf. The grate is of the "dancing horseshoe" type, introduced c.1850.*

249

249. *Cooking ranges with flat tops, completely enclosed fire boxes and built-in ovens were first invented around 1800. They became more and more widely used in some parts of England from about 1850 onwards. This Cornish one is c.1875 but down-hearth cooking continued in some cottages within living memory.*

250

250. *Although a kind of kitchen range, similar to a hob grate, had been devised in the late 18C, it was not until the second half of the 19C that mass produced ranges became the norm. This one of c.1880 is of the open fire box type, particularly favoured in the North of England. It has a large oven (right) and water heating tank with tap (left). Hooks were still being used to suspend kettles or pots over the fire. (Picture: Bill Brocklebank).*

251. *Fireplace in a house of the 1860's with an arched opening and heavy looking brackets to the shelf. It contains a brass firehood of art nouveau period c.1900.*

252

252. *Edwardian fireplace with typical glazed bricks in a livid crimson. The inlaid motif of the frieze and thin shaped shelf brackets are characteristic.*

253

253. *Edwardian fireplace c.1900 with art nouveau repousse metalwork and varnished timber surround. The tall, thin columns and other oddly arranged classical details are all typical.*

254. *Dated cast-iron fireback of the horizontal shape more often seen in the earlier part of the 17C and the late 16C. Note the way in which the patterns have been pressed into the moulding sand to form this rather haphazard repeat. The fleur-de-lys and Tudor rose were very popular motifs. The cast andirons are of a type which persisted from the late 16th. to well into the 17C.*

255. *Bread oven in back wall of 256 (right) with an iron door and latch. The cast-iron fireback is typical of its date (1662), being of wide format, with a shaped top and coat of arms.*

256. *This late 17C kitchen fireplace is being used as a down-hearth as it would have been then. The logs are burned on a bed of ashes on the hearth stone, with a cast-iron fireback to reflect heat and protect the masonry behind. A chimney crane suspends pots over the fire; and a bread oven (see left) is set in the back wall. Andirons: modern but suitable.*

257

257. *The style of this steel, coal burning, basket grate suggests the middle third of the 18C, with its shaped apron and Gothic fret.*

260

260. *This late 18C polished steel grate has side hobs, a Gothic pierced apron and urn finials. It is now a true fitted grate, only pre-dated by a tall, narrow maverick of the late 17th. and early 18C, which quickly disappeared from the scene. The latter are very rare.*

258. *This steel basket grate is of the mid-18C pattern. Note the projected obelisk shaped legs which echo the design of some Elizabethan/Jacobean andirons or dogs. Such "dog grates" as this, developed from the earlier practice of resting a fire basket on the billet bars of traditional dogs.*

261. *This late 18C type of steel grate is pure Adam in design. The tapered legs with spade feet, the swags, urns and anthemion decoration, are all in his manner. In the 18C, the pierced fender originally had no end returns and fitted straight across the opening like this one.*

259. *Late 18C gunmetal basket or dog grate. The influences are those of neo-classical design, with a typical Adam motif in the apron; and characteristic urn finials.*

262. *Another late 18C fitted grate with hobs; but this time the material is cast-iron. The central boss in the surround often contained a key operated spindle for adjusting a smoke shutter to the flue.*

263

263 *Late 18C type of fitted grate with hobs. These served to fill up the fireplace opening, allowing a narrower fire basket. The corner roundels of this one reflect the emerging fashion for these devices in other parts of the house — notably on door architraves.*

264

264,265 & 266. *These pictures show examples of the first phase of cast-iron hob grate manufacture, which started in the late 18C. Many were made by such foundries as Dale, Shropshire and Carron in Falkirk. The front was cast in one piece and the design of opposed semi-circles was typical. However, it precluded any adjustment of width and that proved a disadvantage. Stock sizes varied greatly as a comparison of 264 and 266 shows. The fire basket was placed very high and burned coal at speed.*

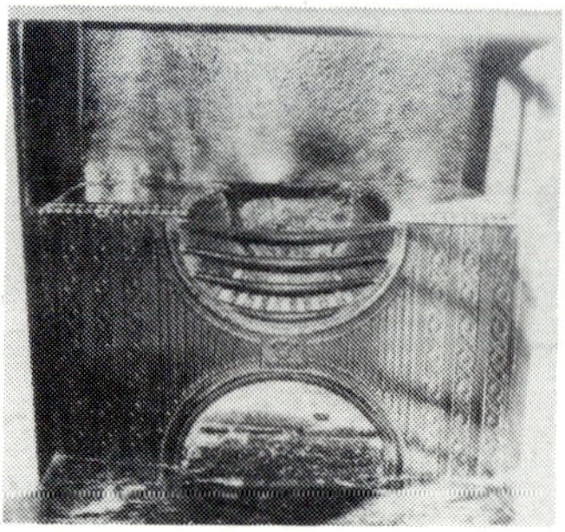

265

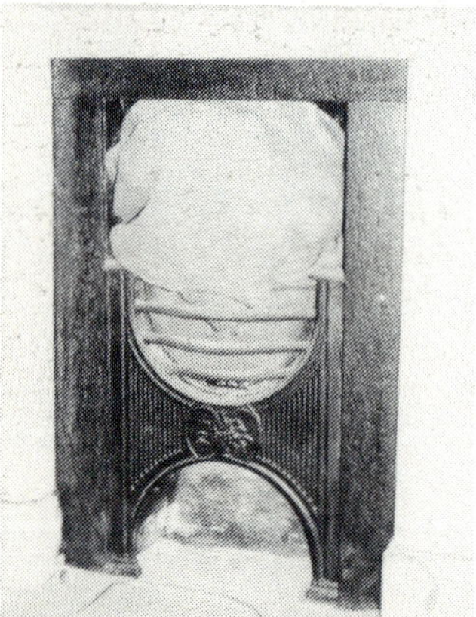

266

267. *This grate of the same period (late 18C) incorporates an adjustable flue shutter to restrict the rate of burning. The ornamental wreath (top centre of surround) contains a round hole for a key. The key turns a spindle and ratchet to open and close a flue shutter.*

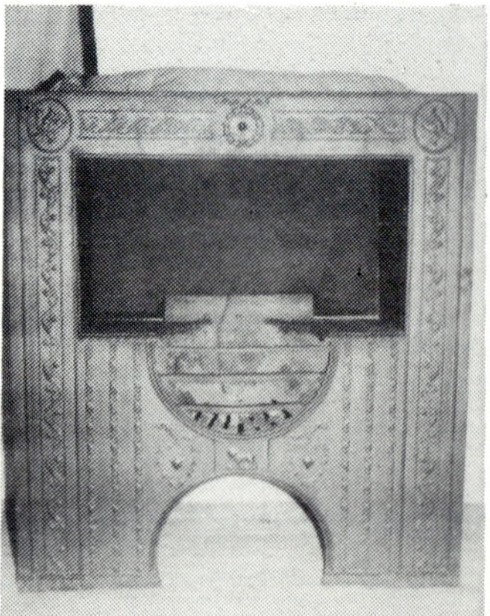

267

268

268. The second phase of hob-grate design took place at the end of the 18C and beginning of the 19C. They cast two separate front plates, usually of ogee outline. The wrought-iron bars of the basket and the apron could then be made longer or shorter, so that the grate would fit the fireplace opening.

269. *This fitted cast-iron grate is a typical early 19C pattern. It has no hobs but is made with very characteristic side columns and finials and has a basket-like arrangement of bars underneath.*

270. *Imagine this plate with doors being substituted for the upper part of 267, so that it rested level with the hobs. Some say this would comprise a form of the original "Bath Stove". It contained the smoke, but doubtless burned furiously when the doors were closed.*

271. *The early 19C sarcophagus grate is a cast-iron affair with burly end standards, shaped at the front like the leg of a console table. The design obviously owes much to the French Empire style.*

272. *An early 19C sarcophagus grate normally has brass mounts and paw feet. Unlike 271 (left) this one has spikes along the top fire bar to stop logs rolling out.*

273. *Phase three in the development of the hob-grate started in the early 19C and disappeared towards 1850, becoming steadily more Victorian in its decoration. The front plates now took the form of rectangular panels with linking wrought fire bars and apron piece. This one in the Nat. Trust's Trerice, is possibly c 1810, since the oval medallions look neo-classical and the fretted apron is similar to earlier steel ones.*

274

274. *Early 19C hob-grate with bowed apron, reeded side panels and anthemion decoration. This one has the "Carron" makers mark cast at the base of the left hand panel, as it should. The fire basket is high above the hearth stone.*

275. *Narrow hob-grates like this one of c 1810-30 were obviously made to fit the fireplaces of lesser bedrooms. The palm leaf design on the convex front plates was a popular French Empire device. Note the firebasket is still placed high up.*

276. *This hob-grate is still more early 19C than anything; but the coarsening of the apron design and the appearance of cast ornament linking the hobs, above the back of the basket, suggest the transitional period of c 1830-50.*

277. *Transitional hob-grate of c1835-50. The apron detail is in the Victorian rococo manner — crisp yet florid. The register plate has now adopted a curved top and spandrels. It has a busy looking decorative motif around the intrados.*

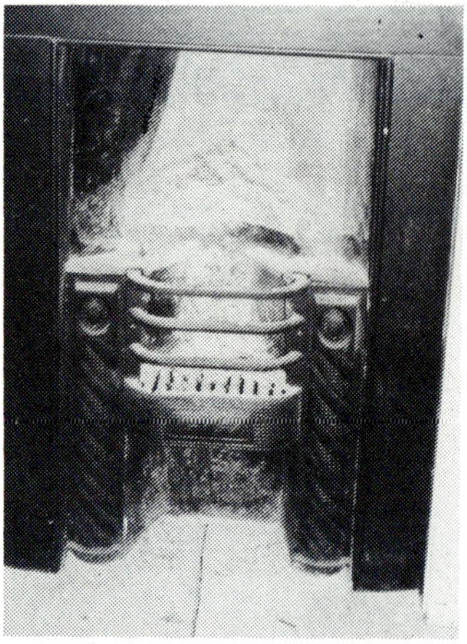

275

276

277

278

278. *The hob-grate is still being made but the decorations in the spandrels of the register plate are typically Victorian, with their bold and somewhat frantic arabesques. A decorative plate joins the back of the hobs. c 1840-55.*

279. *This grate no longer has any hobs. The basket is set high and the curved topped register plate has some decoration of early 19C flavour down the sides. The apron and spandrels however, look thoroughly Victorian. c. 1835-50.*

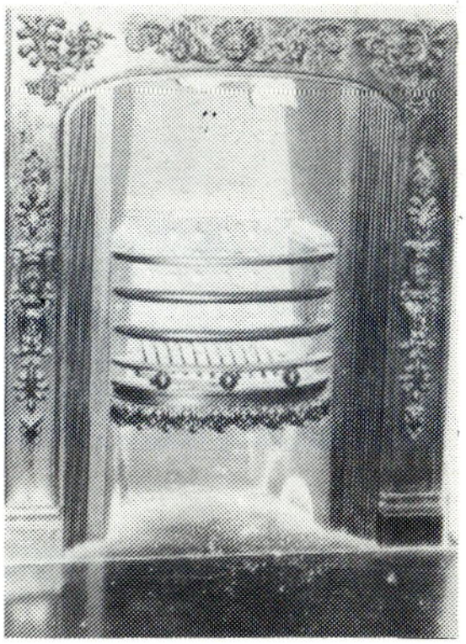

279

280

280. *An example of eclectic Victorian exuberance, this hob-grate design must date c. 1845-55. It has a fine mixture of rococo scrolls (on arch and apron), Jacobean lozenges (on the backplate) and neo-classical panels fronting the hobs.*

281

281. *Although loath to abandon the hobs, the makers of this register grate have introduced the circular arch opening which was to dominate the second half of the 19C. The decoration is a "Jacobethan" riot of oak leaves, acorns, strapwork and arabesques. Probably c 1850-60.*

282. *This design of register grate may be called the "dancing horseshoe" and the example shown is of Carron manufacture dated 1851. Note that the fire basket is now set much lower and hobs are no longert fitted. The decoration is lively but rather vulgar rococo.*

282

283

283. *This cast-iron grate is of the late Victorian period and has a typical arched opening, decorated with a closely repeated anthemion motif. the spandrels have a stylised scroll design of a much more static nature than 278, for example. The shutter for blocking the flue is missing.*

284. *A universal form of cast-iron register grate much employed in the period c. 1860-90. It has a removable shutter giving access to the flue.*

284

285

285. *A style of grate which evolved during the last quarter of the 19C and continued in Edwardian times, included a hood within an arched opening and a characteristic single row of tiles filling the splays on either side.*

286

286. *The principal development of the late Victorian period was the introduction of tiled splays within a rectangular cast iron frame. The tiles are interchangeable; but these are probably a Sherwin and Cotton design from a series depicting stags in Scottish glens, c. 1890. Note that a cast-iron hood has now appeared over the basket, which is set very low.*

TO SUM-UP

The more you look at old buildings and learn to appreciate their subtle details and eccentricities, the clearer it will become that you cannot hope to learn more than a fraction of what you need to know from one small book.

All the same, I hope that this guide will help you to assess what you see in the future, and will prove of practical assistance in dealing with your own house or cottage. With luck, it will tempt you to increase the scope of your reading on such subjects as architectural history, building construction, art and decoration.

The important thing is to train the eye and to be discriminating — capable of enjoying beauty and discerning quality. These two abilities are not, of course, synonymous.

It is inevitable that any book which sets out extensive lists of "do's" and "don'ts" is going to offend or outrage some readers at times. They may also be seen to nod sagaciously when the proffered advice accords with their own actions.

For all that, the idea is not to be provocative, but merely to present a kind of manifesto on how the interiors of old houses may be treated to advantage. I do not really believe that there are many who have lived in seductive old buildings, who will disagree with most of my theory. What they may do is shy at the practical implications as they affect themselves.

I have tried to be as definite and as inclusive as possible, without wandering too far into the realms of interior decoration.

Writing books, however sincere one's motives, is a tiresome business which nobody with any sense undertakes lightly. Still less will a writer gratuitously court the bad opinion of his readers by hurting their feelings. It follows that if one is neither mad nor bad, it is likely that some more or less worthy purpose lies behind the verbiage.

On the whole, I find worthiness a great bore, and my own intentions, while honourable, are also far more selfish and hedonistic.

I love other people to enjoy what I enjoy. The idea that they, and future generations could be missing out on such a fundamental source of happiness is terrible to contemplate. Yet every time an old building is 'modernised' and stripped of its interior features, the owners are wilfully denying themselves and other people, a great deal of pleasure.

The inside of an old house is not a stage set, but rather a setting, in which we work and joke and fend off demons. To function properly it must be an amalgam of atmospheres — the ones we create for ourselves, and those implanted by previous generations.

Some old houses were designed and built for a style of living so different from our own today that they are not entirely amenable to their modern usage. They were intended to be grand places of entertainment and social discourse. They were populous and vital — staffed by numerous servants.

These buildings are, therefore, not necessarily as soulless as we sometimes imagine, when we see them cleared for action on an open day. We look up at the carefully gilded cornice mouldings. Our eyes skim the polished floors, the magnificently restored paintings, the empty chairs behind swagged cords to keep us off the carpets. We are impressed, but slightly dispirited.

Very grand houses were built to contain large numbers of heavily and richly clothed persons and their attendants. People were expected to occupy a good deal of space. Such great rooms occasionally make you feel that they were not proportioned for the whispy, denim-clad dramatis personae of 20th century Britain. Probably these formidable apartments need a good party to make them come alive.

* * * * * * * *

What then are the main principles to be observed when dealing with the interior of an old house or cottage? I think they are as follows:-

We should seek to use natural materials rather than synthetic ones. They will age gracefully, and are rewarding to look at and to touch.

We should distinguish between "rough" and "smooth" buildings. "Rough" ones, like converted barns or cottages, should not be subjected to methods which give them too much finish. It may sometimes be an advantage if you do not employ the most meticulous and conventional craftsmen. These buildings were often slapped together by rough fellows, who had neither the time, expertise or inclination to put a smooth surface or neat edge on everything in sight. Amateur plasterers take heart!

"Smooth" houses however, are another matter. In these it is important that work should be done well. Details and finish should generally be respected.

In all kinds of old buildings, every original feature that can possibly be saved should be left alone, or repaired if it must be.

The temptation is to over-restore, or remake whatever looks tatty and unwholesome. It is a reflex action which should be resisted.

There is no need zealously to preserve ugly additions and embellishments which are not fundamental to the room and its period, just because they are already fairly old.

It is necessary to be selective about being "correct". There may be several "correct" options open to you. Some may be beautiful or pleasing, while others are mean, grisly or overblown. Look at the 18th century pattern books, and you will see that an owner had numerous choices set before him, just as we do. One fireplace may beguile, while another is a squinting abomination. Even the 'beste masters' could have an off-day.

This does not mean, of course, that you take out what is original and integral, but rather that you use good judgement when the opportunity for using it arises.

TO SUM UP

It is vital that every effort is made to avoid repairs or restorations looking faked and unnatural. New work should settle in with a creak and a sigh, so that opening the door of any empty room at the end of the day, you catch it wearing that benign expression which signals success. This is not a mere fancy, and those who have worked with their own hands upon old buildings will know what I mean.

Beware the smug technicians of the old buildings circuit, who know everything and feel nothing. This is by no means to denigrate scholarship and research. They are essential; but must never become a refuge from the awkward necessity for exercising personal taste or judgement.

Sharpen your wits and your ability to see by searching out houses which have not been tampered with, or have retained their integrity.
At the formal end of the scale, Bath Preservation Trust's No 1 The Royal Crescent, is splendid for this purpose, since it has been knowledgeably and sympathetically furnished and restored. There are any number of wonderful old buildings open to the public, either in private hands or administered by organisations like the National Trust.

Visit, learn and enjoy. None are so grand that they may not impart some useful detail or idea for you to use at home.

By our works they shall know us. It is admirable, but relatively easy to preserve a legacy which the wit, taste and energy of our forebears has provided for our delight. These benefits may involve us in a great deal of hard work and expense it is true; but what we must ask in the last event is this:—

Will our own changes, additions and improvements appear equally pleasing in their turn?

TERMS EXPLAINED

ACANTHUS: The leaf of this plant is widely used as a form of decoration in classical architecture, especially for capitals of columns, for arabesques, consoles and cornices. (Fig 72).

ADAM (Robert): Most influential architect and decorator of the second half of the 18th century. His work was chiefly neo-classical. Lived 1728—92.

ADZED: Early methods of converting timber involved sawing boards in a saw pit or splitting them with an iron and beetle. The adze was used to clean up the timber after cutting out. It has a broad, stubby, curved blade set flat on the end of a long wooden handle.

ANCONE: "S"—shaped scrolled bracket or "console", much used in classical architecture, often to support moulded features over doors, windows and fireplaces. (Fig 238).

ANTHEMION: Decorative motif in stylised form of honeysuckle. (Fig 274).

ARABESQUE: A flowing and entwining decoration, usually made up of plant tendrils and leaves. (Fig 8).

ARCH: There are numerous types, but in this book mention is particularly made of the **four-centred** kind (Fig 208). This is the most flattened-out form of the pointed arch (normally 16th or early 17th century). The **segmental** arch forms a segment of a circle. **Flat** arches are not arches at all in shape, but conform with the traditional arch type of construction.

ARCHITRAVE: A moulding in wood or plaster around the sides and head of a door or window opening. (Fig 151). Also serves to decorate and cover the joint between the wall surface and the frame. It is the lowest of the three groups of mouldings which comprise a classical entablature. (See Tuscan Order. Page 19).

ARMATURE: A metal reinforcement securing the larger decorative figures and motifs in plasterwork.

ARRIS: The corner formed by the sharp edge where two wooden, stone or plaster surfaces meet. Vertical edges of a timber post, for example.

ART NOUVEAU: A style of sinuous, flowing decoration, derived from the works of certain designers operating in the 1890's, and before the First World War. (Fig 253).

ARTICLE 4 DIRECTION ORDER: An order procured by a local authority to enable it to limit specific kinds of development which would otherwise be "permitted".

ARTS AND CRAFTS MOVEMENT: An effort to reinstate the guild orientated standards of craftsmanship and design of Medieval Europe. William Morris was one of its leaders.

ASTRAGAL: A small rounded moulding like a bead — almost cylindrical. Also used to denote glazing bars of cabinet doors.

ATLANTES: Male figures used like 'caryatids' to support a classical entablature.

ATTIC BASE: Base of a column with two torus mouldings separated by "fillets" and a "scotia" mould.

BALUSTER: The wooden, stone or metal uprights supporting a staircase handrail between newel posts. Often of barley sugar, vase or column shape. (Fig 191).

BALUSTRADE: The whole assembly of handrail, "newels" and "balusters" which flank a landing or staircase.

BANISTER: The same as a baluster — common usage.

BAROQUE: A style of architecture and decoration which uses the classical language in a grand but lively way. The features have movement; pediments are broken; the eye is led upwards. There are curves and counter-curves.

BASKET GRATE: A free standing iron basket, burning logs and, later, coals. Most early ones were fairly plain. Those by Robert Adam, for instance, were most sophisticated. See also "Dog Grate". (Figs 257—261).

BAY LEAF GARLAND: Decorative moulding, usually seen on convex friezes and ceilings. Consists of tightly bundled bay leaves wound about with ribbon. (Fig 58).

BEAD: A small linear convex moulding. Beads are usually run in closely spaced groups on features like architraves. (Fig 130).

BEAD & REEL: A popular form of enrichment for lengths of rounded moulding. Cylinders alternate with bobbins. (Fig 9).

BEAM: A structural timber of substantial section mainly used to support floor joists (Fig 43), or to tie the feet of principal roof rafters together, thus forming a roof truss.

BED MOULDING: The mouldings which run below a decorative projection, like the upper part of a classical cornice. i.e. The "cyma recta" and "corona" are "bedded" on a group of mouldings underneath. (See Tuscan Entablature. Page 19).

BELFAST SINK: Trough shaped white "stoneware" sink, used in kitchens and sculleries. Typical size: 24x18x10ins.

BELL FLOWER: Popular 18th century flower decoration strung together to form drops or swags, and also used to enrich convex mouldings. (Fig 232).

BEVEL: To cut the edge off a piece of timber or stone so that it then slants at more or less than 45 deg. is to bevel it. A symmetrical cut of 45 deg. is a "chamfer". ("Mouldings" page 18).

BOISERIE: Panelling decorated with carved or moulded designs in the French manner of Louis XIV, XV and XVI. (Fig 29).

BOLECTION MOULDING: Usually used around wall or door panels, but also fireplaces, this moulding stands proud of the framing members and is often shaped in a double curve or "ogee". (Fig 231 and "Mouldings" page 18).

BOSS: A carved or moulded ornamental block covering the intersection of beams or ceiling ribs. (Figs 40 and 41).

BUILDING REGULATIONS: Statutory regulations (of some complexity), obliging those who carry out various types of building work to apply for consent from the Local Authority, submit plans and have the works inspected. Pay great attention to these.

BRACKET: A support, decorative or otherwise, for projecting features like cornices and shelves (Fig 249). Often "S" shaped. On the cut string of a staircase it is purely ornamental. (Fig 144, 180, 192 etc).

BUCRANIA: Decorative ox skulls, usually linked with swags.

BUN FINIAL: Ornamental bun-shaped projection on top of a newel post. (Fig 173).

CAMBERED LINTEL: Usually across a fireplace opening, this runs slightly upwards towards the centre. Often contrived from natural shape of a piece of timber. (Fig 207).

CAMES: Lead strips which hold the glass panes in lead-glazed windows. (Fig 15).

CAMP CEILING: An attic type ceiling which follows the line of the rafters at the sides and is flat across the middle of the room.

CARYATIDS: Female figures used to support a classical entablature.

CAP: Short form for the word "capital" used to describe the group of mouldings at the top of a feature like a pilaster, pier or newel. (Figs 154 and 35).

CAPITAL: The top part of any column where it spreads out to take the load. It is ornamented with carving or mouldings according to its style and period. Also the top of a pilaster — especially a classical one. (See Tuscan Order. Page 19).

CASEMENT: A window which is side-hung to open outwards in Britain, and inwards in European countries. (Figs 7 and 15).

CASTING: The process of making an object by pouring a material, which will later solidify, into a specially prepared mould.

CAST-IRON: Ironwork made by "casting", as above.

CAVETTO: A moulding which curves inwards, often in quarter circle. (See "Mouldings" page 18)

CHAIR RAIL: A moulded wood or plaster decoration which equates with the uppermost moulding of a classical pedestal. It runs around the walls of a room at a level which might prevent the backs of chairs from doing damage to the finishes. (See "Parts of a Room" page 17).

CHAMFER: See bevel. On beams and lintels etc. usually 17th century, or earlier. ("Mouldings" page 18 and Fig 46).

CHASE: A channel cut in a wall to carry pipes or wiring, etc.

CHEVRON: A zig-zag ornament, much used around Norman arches.

CHIMNEY CRANE: A braced iron bar which is hinged to the side of an open hearth and can be swung across the fire to suspend cooking pots. (Fig 256).

CHINOISERIE: Decoration using Chinese motifs like pagodas, wooden bridges, exotic birds and dragons. Fashionable in late 17th and 18th centuries. Often includes Rococo influences.

CLOAM OVEN: Manufactured earthenware oven normally built into the wall near or inside the hearth. The oven was pre-heated with a fire of furze, raked out, and the dough was then sealed up for baking by replacing the loose door and sealing it around with clay. (Fig 208a).

CLOSED-STRING STAIRCASE: Strings are the main framing members forming the sides of a staircase. In a "closed-string" type the treads are housed into the strings. In an "open string" the shape of the stairs is cut out and the treads rested on the string. "Wall string" is fixed to the wall of the stair well. (Fig 180 etc.)

COCK'S HEAD HINGE: Iron or brass "H"-hinge with ends like cocks' heads. Mainly 17th century. (Fig 166).

COLLAR: Horizontal timber spiked or pegged to each pair of rafters to stop them pulling apart under load. "Camp ceilings" often fixed to these.

COMPOSITE ORDER: Classical Roman order which combines the Ionic capital with the Corinthian one.

CONSOLE: As for "Ancone" see above. (Fig 238).

CONTINUED CHIMNEYPIECE: A large, classically inspired chimneypiece, which extends right up the wall to form an architectural feature with bold cornice or pediment. (Fig 234).

CORBEL: A stone or timber support which projects from a wall to carry the load of a structural member such as a beam.

CORINTHIAN ORDER: The classical order of architecture with column capitals freely decorated with acanthus leaves. The cornice may be identified by its scrolled "modillion" brackets. (Figs 8 and 9).

CORNICE: The uppermost of the three parts of a classical "entablature". Composed of several mouldings, usually with a "fillet" and "cyma recta" at the top. (See Tuscan Entablature page 19).

CORONA: Flat, vertical band forming middle area of cornice. (See page 19).

COVE: A substantial concave moulding often used like a cornice to join the walls to the ceiling. (Fig 81)

CROCKETS: Curled over knob-like ornaments of flower or leaf derivation, used to decorate ogee hood moulds in Gothic architecture. (Fig 157).

CROSS GARNET: Strap hinge hung on a gudgeon pin. (Figs 130, 131, 137).

CROWN GLASS: Glass blown into a disc was cut out to form crown glass window panes. The main method until the 1830's. (Fig 17).

CURTAIL STEP: The bottom step of a staircase which is projected sideways and curled around, like a 'cur's tail'. (fig 197 etc.)

CUSP: Gothic tracery often took form of trefoil or quatrefoil ornament. A quatrefoil is composed of four curves. Where they join, they form "cusps". (Fig 28).

CUT-STRING: See "closed-string". (Fig 193 etc.)

CYMA RECTA: This moulding is like an asymmetrical and flattened out "S", with the hollow curve uppermost. "Cyma reversa" has the hollow at the bottom.

DADO RAIL: See "chair rail" above. (See page 17).

DADO: That part of a wall's panelling, or other decoration, which equates with the main area between top and bottom mouldings of a classical "pedestal". (See "Parts of a Room" page 17 and "Tuscan Entablature" page 19).

DENTILS: Small, square ornamental blocks seen in the cornices of Ionic, Composite and Corinthian orders. (fig 73).

DISTRESS: To age a material artificially by such means as scoring, denting, chipping or staining.

TERMS EXPLAINED

DOG GRATE: A free-standing iron or steel basket grate incorporating a cast fireback and pronounced front legs. Clearly derived from fire dogs. Mainly 18th century. (Fig 258 etc.)

DOG LEG STAIRCASE: The first flight ends at a half-landing and then doubles back in a second flight which finishes the ascent. The outer string of the second flight is directly above the first, or very nearly so.

DOORCASE: All that joinery work which frames, surrounds and adorns a door opening.

DORIC ORDER: The simplest of the three Greek Orders of Architecture.

DOWN-HEARTH: A fireplace in which the fire is burned upon a bed of ashes actually on the hearthstone, sometimes with the help of firedogs. (Fig 256).

DUCK'S NEST GRATE: Like a hob grate but much lower and less elegant. Sometimes portable and associated with 18th and early 19th century kitchens.

EGG AND DART MOULDING: A row of egg shaped ornaments, divided up by little arrow or tongue motifs. Used to embellish small convex mouldings. (Fig 88).

EMPIRE STYLE: The early 19th century style of design largely derived from neo-classical and Egyptian details, the latter brought back by Napoleon from North Africa.

ENCAUSTIC TILES: Patterned earthenware — normally glazed. Much favoured by Victorian and Edwardian builders. (Fig 116).

ENTABLATURE: The topmost horizontal element in a classical order. Consists of a cornice, frieze and architrave, reading downwards.

ESCUTCHEON: In door furniture, it is the ornamental and protective plate which surrounds the keyhole.

FANLIGHT: Glazed light above a door, often fan-shaped and ornamented; but the term is applied to the rectangular kind of light as well.

FASCIA: Classical architraves consist of one or more horizontal flat bands called fascias. From these derive modern fascia boards, below the eaves.

FESTOON: Carved or moulded swag of flowers or fruit, etc.

FIELDED PANEL: A wall or door panel with a raised centre area which is sloped off, bevelled or "fielded" around the sides. (Fig 22).

FILLETS: Plain narrow bands in wood, stone or plaster which divide more shapely mouldings from each other. (See Tuscan Order page 19).

FIRE-DOGS: Have relatively small iron billet-bars, and are three-legged, with upstand ("Stauke") at front end. Dogs are used for resting logs while they burn. Smaller than "andirons". Sometimes called "brand irons" or "creepers". (Fig 254).

FINIAL: Usually a turned or carved ornament in the shape of an urn, ball, bun, spike or figure which was often used to decorate staircase newel posts. (Fig 178, etc).

FIRE PRECAUTIONS ACT: Act which embodies legislation demanding various standards of fire safety in buildings with a public use, like hotels and offices, etc. It is enforced and interpreted by local fire officers (complex and often detrimental to old houses).

FINISHES: The surfaces which the eye encounters — floor tiles, plaster, paint, gilding, marble.

FIREBACK: A portable cast-iron slab of more or less elaborate design which stands at the back of the hearth to protect the wall and help reflect heat. Long, low shapes tend to be 16th century; and outline becomes increasingly upright and Baroque in decoration throughout 17th century. (Fig 254, 255 etc.)

FIREHOOD: A form of canopy in metal, plaster, brick or stone, to stand right over the fire and funnel smoke into the flue of a big open hearth. (Fig 219, 247, 253).

FLEURON: A stylised flower decoration often used to punctuate the corners of door, fireplace and ceiling mouldings. (Fig 87 and 159).

FLUE: The interior of the chimney through which the smoke passes. Old ones often leak and need lining.

FLUTING: Parallel concave channels usually decorating a column, pilaster or architrave (Fig 6). They are sometimes divided by fillets and sometimes by arrises.

FLUSH DOOR: Plain, smooth door, constructed with either a solid or hollow core, surfaced with plywood or other laminates.

FREESTONE: Fine grained stone which can be worked in any direction; and is relatively easy to carve or cut with a saw. Normally limestone or sandstone.

FRIEZE: The middle element of the three which compose a classical entablature. Often decorated with arabesques, etc. (Fig 83 and 84. etc and page 19).

GEOMETRIC STAIRCASE: Usually a cantilevered staircase which winds up around an open well, the steps being rested upon each other and unsupported at their outer ends (Fig 194). Either circular or elliptical in plan.

GESSO: Made from gypsum or chalk with glue to bind it, this is used as a dense white base for the decoration of panelling and for gilded mouldings. Hates damp.

GILDING: Gold or other metallic leaf is applied like a transfer to a surface coated with sticky gold-size.

GOING: The total depth of stair tread, from front to back, upon which you can place your foot, less the projection of one "nosing". (See "Parts of a Staircase" page 17).

GOTHIC: The architectural style of the Middle Ages, from rougly 1200 to 1500 which is typified by the use of the pointed arch. Much 16th and even 17th century, work is also Gothic in spirit or detail.

GOTHIC REVIVAL: First revival, often called "Strawberry Hill Gothic" started c.1750 (Horace Walpole). Then Regency Gothic, in early 19th century. Finally, Victorian Gothic (Pugin, et al.) from 1840's.

GREEK REVIVAL: Style of architecture and design which embraced pure classical Greek models rather than those derived from Renaissance Roman forms. Took hold in the late 18th and early 19th centuries.

GRIP FLOOR: Mixture of beaten lime and ash, normally used as a ground floor, but sometimes laid upstairs on laths supported by joists.

GRIP HANDRAIL: Heavily made Elizabethan or Jacobean handrail with a pronounced roll moulding on the top.

GRISAILLE: Glass or painted panels normally classical in manner in monochromatic tones. (See page 42)

GUILLOCHE: A decorative design of continuous interlacing circles. (Fig 90).

GUTTAE: Drop-like ornaments which occur below the "triglyphs" in the Doric Order. Sometimes under sills or stair brackets. (Fig 193).

"H"-HINGE: A predominant hinge used in the 17th and much of the 18th century which was always nailed, not screwed. (Fig 166).

HANGING STILE: Door's vertical framing member on the hinged side. (See "Parts of a Room" page 17).

HOB GRATE: Cast-iron coal burning grate. Late 18th century onwards. Three main types. (Fig 262 — 268 and 273 — 278 also 281).

INGLE NOOK FIREPLACE: A large open fireplace with a "down-hearth" and a built-in seat, or seats, inside the chimneybreast. Often 16th or 17th century. (Fig 207 and 220).

INLAID FLOOR: A kind of parquet of wood strips laid with, and against, the grain. Sometimes term is used to describe a marquetry floor. Seldom is decoration truly inlaid into the actual carcase timber.

INTRADOS: The inner curve of an arch.

IONIC ORDER: The Classical order with bold volutes to the column capitals but no acanthus leaves. Has dentil decoration in the cornice. (Fig 6).

JACOBEAN ARCHITECTURE: The English Renaissance style of the early 17th century, embodying a mixture of elaborate decoration, Gothic in spirit, with what are sometimes rather crude efforts at the classical orders. (Figs 6, 8, 51, 211, 218, etc.)

JAMBS: The stones, bricks or posts which form the vertical sides of an opening. (Fig 212, etc.)

JIB DOOR: A disguised door fitted within the panelling of a wall, and seeming to be part of it. (fig 155).

JOINERY: The finishing woodwork in a house, e.g. doors, stairs and panelling. Also the fitting and making of such items.

JOIST: The smaller section timbers which carry floor boards. Joists are further supported by "beams", if required. (Figs 43 and 97).

KEY PATTERN: A meander-like fret of Greek origin, used as a decoration. (Fig 83).

KEYSTONE: Centre stone of an arch.

KNEE AND RAMP: Staircase handrail forms a sharp "knee" and is "ramped" down to the level of the next flight of steps. (See "Parts of a Staircase"). Also, see "Swan-neck".

"L"-HINGE: Typical 17th and early 18th century hinge. (Fig 145 and 153).

LATH AND PLASTER: Timber framed partitions (and external walls of some buildings) are covered with closely spaced thin strips of wood (Laths) which act as a key for a plaster finish. (Fig 10).

LEDGED DOOR: Door of vertical boards nailed to others placed horizontally. (Fig 136 and 137).

LEDGED AND BRACED DOOR: As above, but with diagonal boards nailed between ledges, to brace the door and prevent sagging. (Fig 165).

LINENFOLD: Panel decoration carved to look like stylised folds of fabric. Usually Tudor (Fig 1).

LINTEL: A structural component, usually of timber, stone or concrete, which carries the load over a window, door or fireplace opening. (Fig 206, 207, 212 etc.).

LISTED BUILDING: Building listed by the D.O.E. as of Architectural or Historic interest. Three grades: I, II star and II, in that order of importance. Buildings are protected by law (inside and out) against unauthorised demolition, or work which adversely affects the "character".

LOZENGE: A diamond shaped decoration, often of Jacobean panelling.

MASK: Decoration in form of a face, sometimes "grotesque". (Fig 24).

MASON'S MITRE: Method of returning a moulding around a panel, or similar feature in stone or wood. (Fig 1).

MAST NEWEL STAIRCASE: Spiral stair with timber treads housed into a central post, which rises up through the building or an attached turret or wing. (Fig 172).

MEDALLION: Decorative oval or circle, often containing a head or figure in relief, or sometimes a painting.

METOPE: The gaps in Doric frieze between triglyphs, often containing relief ornament.

MITRE: At corners, mouldings like architraves are sawn to butt together at 45 deg.

MODILLIONS: scrolled brackets placed horizontally under the corona of a classical cornice — should be Corinthian or Composite. (Fig 82)

MORTICE: A slot cut out of a framing timber to house a tenon, thus forming an effective joint.

MOULDINGS: Shaped lengths of great variety in plaster, stone or wood, used as ornament, weathering and for the concealment of joints between one building surface and another. (see drawings page 18)

MUFF GLASS: Muff or cylinder glass was blown in cylinder form, slit lengthways and unrolled into flat pieces from which window panes could be cut.

MULLIONS: Stone or timber uprights, dividing window openings vertically into separate 'lights'. (Figs 7 and 9)

MUNTIN: The intermediate upright framing members in doors or panelling.(see 'parts of a room' page 17)

MUTULES: Decorative blocks fixed beneath the corona of the Doric cornice.

NEO-CLASSICAL: The type of design which became popular in the second half of the 18C. It was derived from ancient Roman and Greek forms observed at first hand by architects, travellers and archaeologists. One of the most important was Johann Winckelmann (1717-68). Also Robert Adam.

NEWEL: A structural post in stone, metal or wood, supporting a balustrade at the top, bottom and changes of direction in a staircase. (see "Parts of a Staircase" page 17)

NEWEL STAIR: A spiral staircase in timber or stone. (Fig 168)

NICHE: A wall recess for a statue, bust or shelves. Often has an arched top. (Fig 35)

TERMS EXPLAINED

NOGGING: Short lengths of timber fixed between the vertical studs of a partition to stiffen the construction. In timber framed houses bricks used to fill the space between posts are "brick nogging".

NOSING: The part of a stair tread which projects beyond the riser. (See "Parts of a Staircase" page 17).

OGEE MOUDLING: An "S" shaped section — cyma recta or reversa.

OPEN-WELL STAIRCASE: Staircase rising in relatively short flights around a well. Has quarter-landings, and earliest are 16th century. (Figs 171, 178, 182).

ORDERS OF ARCHITECTURE: The formal system of classical design in architecture started by the Greeks, adapted by the Romans and re-interpreted in the Italian Renaissance. Without some basic study of the Orders, little sense can be made of architecture and interiors. (See "Tuscan Order" page 19).

ORMOLU: Either gilded bronze ornamental mounts, door furniture, etc; or a metal alloy formed mainly of copper with some zinc and tin.

OVERMANTEL: The upper part of a chimneypiece above the level of the mantel-shelf. Usually consists of a panel topped by cornice or pediment, sometimes flanked by volutes or pilasters. (Figs.235,236).

OVOLO: Small quarter-round convex moulding. ("Mouldings" page 18).

PAINTED FLOOR: Type of floor decoration favoured in 18th century; but original examples are very rare.

PALLADIAN: Architecture and design based upon Andrea Palladio's 16th century Renaissance buildings and versions of the Roman Orders. Exceptionally influential in English 17th and 18th century work.

PALMETTE: A small repeated ornament used to decorate late 18th century moulded plasterwork. Like a palm leaf, but easily confused with an "anthemion".

PANELLED DOOR: Door framed with stiles, rails and muntins and filled in with panels. Earliest tend to be 17th century in Britain. (Figs 145, 157 etc).

PATERA: Small disc-like ornament, round or oval particularly favoured by Neo-Classical designers, like Robert Adam. Often seen on fireplaces and plaster friezes. (Figs 83, 232, 241).

PEDESTAL: The rectangular base structure upon which a classical column sometimes stands. Also for statues. (See "Tuscan Order", page 19).

PEDIMENT: A triangular (or sometimes segmental) feature of timber, stone or plaster which forms the topmost element of a classical door, window or fireplace (Fig 145, 146, 234, 235 etc.)

PENDANT: A form of decorative boss formed as a downward extension of the ribs in Elizabethan and Jacobean ceilings (Fig 45). Also Gothic. Used, also, to decorate bottom of staircase newel. (Fig 178 and 184).

PERMITTED DEVELOPMENT: Certain types of minor works which may be carried out without Planning Permission.

PILASTER: A flattened out rectangular version of a column attached to the wall, more for decoration than structure. (Fig 6, 8, 18).

PLANTED MOULDING: A wooden moulding applied to a surface rather than one shaped from the framing itself.

PLINTH BLOCK: Block at skirting level which finishes a door or fireplace architrave. ("Parts of a Room", page 17).

POST: An upright structural timber of generous section. (Fig 43 — at foot of Staircase).

PRINCIPAL RAFTERS: In a roof these form a series of "trusses" carrying purlins, which in their turn, support the smaller common rafters. Often left exposed in attic rooms. (Fig 3).

PULVINATED FRIEZE: Frieze of convex section. Often used for fireplaces and overdoors. (Fig 64, 148 etc).

PURLIN: Structural timber running lengthways along a roof, of roughly square section. Transfers load of common rafters to the roof trusses. (Fig 3).

QUADRANT MOULD: Moulding of quarter circle section. Also called "ovolo".

QUARRY TILES: Unglazed, burnt clay tiles. Non-porous. Usually red. (Fig 115, 117).

RAFTERS: (common rafters) These carry the battens or laths from which the roof tiles or slates are hung. Rafters rest on purlins which transfer the load to the roof trusses. (Fig 3).

RAILS: The horizontal framing members in door or panelling construction. ("Parts of a Room", page 17).

REBATE: Step-shaped recess cut from a piece of timber. e.g. Picture frame is "rebated" to take glass. ("Mouldings" page 18).

REEDING: Closely spaced half-round beading often used in 19th century architraves. ("Mouldings" page 18).

REGISTER GRATE: A cast iron or sheet metal plate fills the main fireplace opening. The plate itself has a diminished opening for a relatively small fitted grate. Normally second half of 19th century. (Fig 231, 282, 283, 284)

REGISTER PLATE: Metal plate which fits and seals an opening like that of a fireplace or flue.

RENDERING: First coat of plaster on a solid wall. Sometimes the only coat. When used on laths it should strictly be called a "pricking-up" coat.

RETURN: When a wall or moulding changes direction at right-angles. Adequate "returns" are visually vital at the sides of openings.

REVEAL: The visible exterior part of a window jamb, between frame and main wall surface.

RIBS: A projecting band on a ceiling. Elizabethan and Jacobean plasterwork is usually made up of "ribbed" designs. Also the structural "ribs" of vaulting. (Fig 45, 45a, 51, 52).

RIM LOCK: Metal cased lock screwed or bolted to face of door. (Fig 167c).

RIVEN FLAGSTONES: Flagstones which have been split and show a "riven" face rather than a sawn one.

RISER: The vertical face of a step. ("Parts of a Staircase" page 17).

ROSETTE: Decorative device, normally round, using a stylised flower motif. (Figs 77, 88).

ROCOCO: A style of decoration using freely flowing designs of "C" and "S" scrolls, foliage, shells and arabesques. Popular in England during the middle third of the 18th.C. Very elegant and frivolous. (Fig 80

SASH WINDOW: (double-hung) Window with suspended sashes, opened and closed by vertical movement, within a box frame. (Fig 17).

SARCOPHAGUS GRATE: Early 19th century cast-iron grate, with marked horizontal emphasis. Has solid back and slab-like ends, which are shaped and decorated with brass mounts in the Empire manner. (Fig 271, 272).

SCAGLIOLA: A type of highly polished imitation marble composition. Often late 18th century and much favoured for columns and chimneypieces.

SCOTIA MOULD: Concave moulding like a "cavetto" but less symmetrical. ("Mouldings" page 18).

SCREED: A layer of mortar used to level-up and provide a smooth floor surface upon which to lay finishes. Usually one or two inches thick.

SCREENS PASSAGE: Passage formed at the lower end of a medieval hall by screening off the main area from the exterior door. Often minstrels' gallery over.

SLIPS: Well finished rectangular slabs which immediately surround the fireplace opening. ("Parts of a Room", page 17).

SMOKE SHUTTER: Shutter of steel, glass or some other incombustible material, used to lower the smoke-line of a fireplace opening and prevent smoke leaking into the room. (Fig 211).

SMOKE HOOD: See "Fire-hood".

SNECK: Lever for lifting a latch. Sneck-latch is traditional in old houses of many types and periods. (Fig 136, 137).

SOFFIT: The underside of window openings, beams, closed staircases, etc. (Fig 7).

SPANDREL: The triangular area formed between an arch and the rectangular opening in which it is placed. (Fig 149, 205, 208).

SPLAY: When the interior jambs of a window opening are opened out instead of being at right angles to the wall surface, they are called "splays".

STEEL TROWEL FINISH: A smooth plaster finish to wall or to a mortar floor screed.

STILES: The outermost vertical framing members of a system or panelling, and in the same way, of a door. ("Parts of a Room", page 17).

STOCK-LOCK: Like a rim lock it is screwed or bolted to door, but has a hardwood case. (Fig 125, 139, 167a).

STOPPED-CHAMFER: When the lower edge of a beam, for example, ceases to be chamfered off, it is said to be "stopped".For this purpose various decorative mouldings are used to effect the change from "chamfer" to plain rectangular section. (figs 42, 44, 46).

STRAP-HINGE: Iron band nailed or bolted to a door and curled around at one end to fit over a gudgeon pin, fixed to the jamb or frame. (fig 130. 131, 134, 137,etc.)

STRAPWORK: Strictly, banded decoration in the form of leather straps. (Fig 209). Brought to Britain in late 16th and early 17th century pattern books from the Low Countries and Germany (Vredeman de Vries et al). Loosely used to describe "Jacobean" ceilings with flat, decorated rib-work. (Fig 51).

STRING: See "Closed-String Staircase" and Fig 173.

STRIP FLOORING: Narrow floor boards laid in random lengths often on a solid sub-floor. (Fig 111).

STRUT: In old houses, normally a fairly short piece of timber used to hold two other structural timbers apart. (Fig 3d).

STUCK MOULDINGS: Those which are formed on a piece of timber and are therefore integral to it, rather than mouldings which are run in separate lengths and applied afterwards.

STUDS: Vertical timbers, evenly spaced, to form the frame of a parition or wall. (Fig 3, 10).

SUNK PANEL: One with its surface lying below that of the surrounding framework. (Figs 5, 6, 21, 25).

SWAG: A decorative garland of foliage, fruit or flowers, etc., as if suspended between two points. (Figs 9, 24, 84).

SWAN-NECK: Term for a component like a wall coping, pediment or hand rail which adopts an ogee curve. (Figs 145, 182, 235).

TENON: End of a piece of timber cut away to fit into a "mortice". Extensivly used framing joint.

TERMS: Used like a column or pilaster, these supports comprise a human head and torso merging into a downward tappering pedestal.

THUMB LATCH: Or "Norfolk" latch. Has a grip handle and thumb piece for pushing up the sneck, which goes through the door, and lifts the latch on other side. (page 38.)

TIE BEAM: Substantial beam, spanning from wall to wall, which ties together the feet of the principal rafters, thus forming a roof truss.

TOP RAIL: The uppermost horizontal framing member in a system of panelling. ("Parts of a Room", page 17).

TORCHING: Traditionally, lime mortar pointing used to seal the heads of slates or tiles inside a roof space. But also, by derivation, describes the all over plastering of the backs of the slating laths between common rafters.

TORUS MOULDING: Sometimes called "bull-nosed" this is a bold convex moulding, used on steps, sills and at the bases of columns. ("Mouldings" page 18).

TRIGLYPH: Frieze decoration consisting of two vertical channels, flanked by a half-channel on either side. Always Doric.

TRIMMER: A floor joist which carries the ends of other joists which have been cut off to form an opening for a staircase or fire hearth.

TRIMMING JOISTS: Joists of increased thickness which carry the ends of the "trimmer joist" of a staircase or fire hearth opening.

TRUSS: Roof trusses consist of pairs of rafters, tied with a horizontal member to form a triangle.

TUSCAN ORDER: The robust looking Roman simplification of the Doric Order. Has no fluting, no frieze decoration and has a torus moulding between two fillets, instead of an attic base. (See page 19).

VANITAS THEME: Dutch and Flemish 17C still life painters employed a variety of symbols to denote the transience of life, and the futility of storing up treasure on earth. The hour-glass or a watch represented the passage of time. "Vanitas" means emptiness in Latin.

TERMS EXPLAINED

VENETIAN WINDOW: Window with a round arch head, closely flanked by lower and narrower flat-headed lights. Palladian.

VITRUVIAN SCROLL: A running wave decoration of classical origin. (Fig 24)

VOLUTE: A decorative scroll feature seen in the capitals of Ionic, Corinthian and Composite columns. Also used large for facades of Renaissance and Baroque churches. (Fig 234)

VOUSSOIRS: The snugly fitting cut stones which form an arch.

WAINSCOTTING: Another name for wall panelling.

WALL-STRING: See "closed-string".

WREATHED HANDRAIL: One which curls around to form a decorative termination over the bottom newel post of a staircase. (Fig 194, 197). Also, single and double-twist wreaths to carry handrail around a stairwell.

WROUGHT-IRON: Ironwork which has been shaped while hot from the fire of a blacksmith's forge. Also a high quality iron for this purpose.

WOOD FLOAT FINISH: Plaster textured to give a slightly roughened effect by working it over before it sets with a wooden version of the steel trowel.

THE AUTHOR

The writer is a specialist in matters connected with old buildings. On leaving Marlborough, he trained first as a journalist with a provincial evening newspaper. Later, he worked for a well-known London magazines group and then as a press officer.

After moving to the West Country, from which his father's family originates, he qualified in building construction, becoming an Associate of the Chartered Institute of Building. From the outset, he has directed his interests towards the history, protection and repair of old houses and cottages.

He works as an architectural journalist and author; and practices as a consultant on the structural problems, restoration and decoration of old buildings. He also lectures groups, and classes in further education, on these and allied subjects.